FABERGÉ

from St Petersburg to Sandringham

This book is for Alexandra Hunter, born 6 April 2017

Fabergé from St Petersburg to Sandringham

Ian Collins
Sainsbury Centre for Visual Arts

This publication accompanies the exhibition
Royal Fabergé
Curated by Ian Collins
Sainsbury Centre for Visual Arts
14 October 2017–11 February 2018

Sainsbury Centre for Visual Arts
UEA
Norwich NR4 7TJ
www.scva.ac.uk

ISBN: 978-0-9460-0971-8

Printed and bound by Swallowtail Press, Norwich

The Sainsbury Centre and The Russia Season are supported by:

A LA VIEILLE RUSSIE

Front/back cover
FABERGÉ
Cigarette case *c.* 1910
Gold, enamel, rose diamonds
A LA VIEILLE RUSSIE, NEW YORK

FABERGÉ

from St Petersburg to Sandringham

IAN COLLINS

Family Tree

showing the key links between the British, Danish and Russian Royal houses

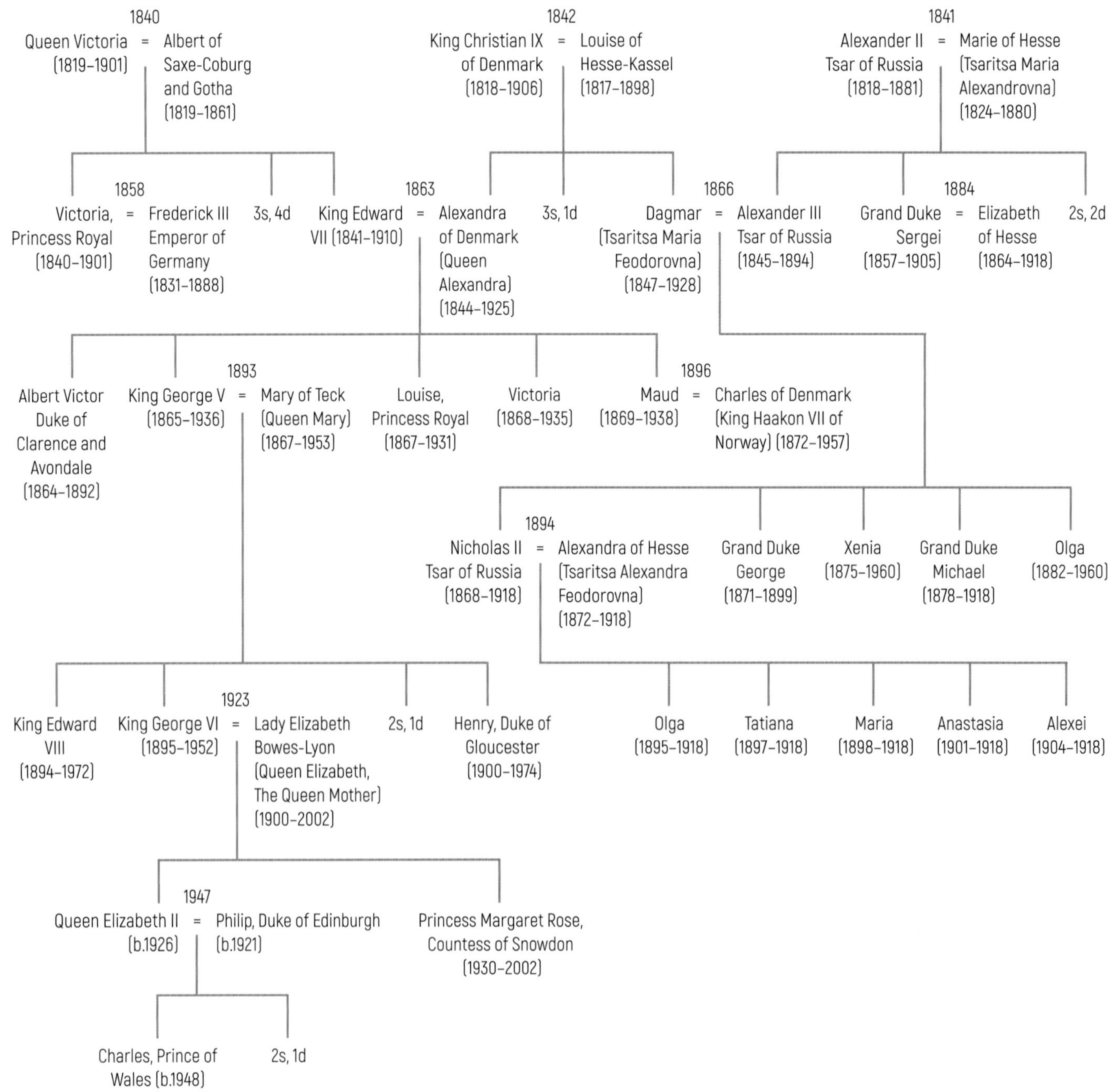

Contents

All chapters take the titles of short stories by the Russian master Anton Chekhov.

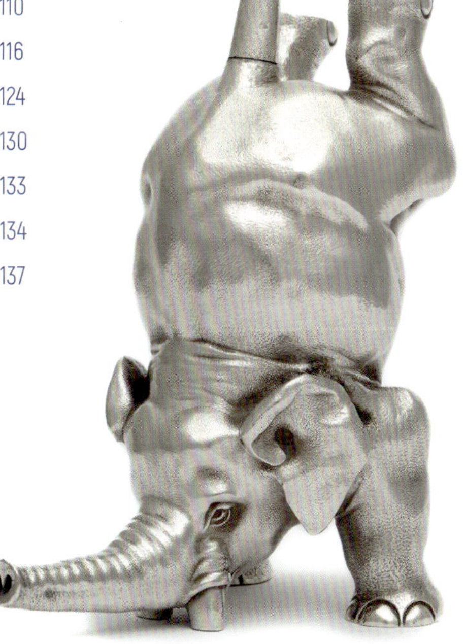

FABERGÉ
Elephant stamp moistener *c.* 1895
Silver
h. 102 mm
A LA VIEILLE RUSSIE, NEW YORK

The elephant is the symbol of the Danish Royal Family. This stamp moistener holds glue in its body and has a brush in its tail.

PREFACE

Art

During the course of a glittering career in imperial Russia, between 1882 and 1917, Peter Carl Fabergé (1846–1920) is thought to have directed the design and production of around 200,000 exquisite artefacts. They divided, roughly equally, into three categories: jewellery, silver wares and small-scale *objets d'art*. While many of these things have come down to us, still more were lost during and after the Bolshevik Revolution. Much was broken up and melted down. The items that survived did so because the craftsmanship was deemed to be worth more than the materials and they could be sold abroad for hard currency.

These small, majestic works of art have a bitter-sweet aura. Relics of intense and tragic times, they show us that beyond the grand oppositions that formed the age in which they were made – war and peace, wealth and poverty, imperialism and revolution, love and death – what survives is art.

Fabergé was in the middle of, and deeply affected by, a monumental shift in the relationship between Britain and Russia. On 31 August 1907 the Anglo-Russian Convention was signed in St Petersburg, tying the two traditional enemies politically. At the same time, through a spectacular commission, the British monarchy brought them together culturally. The Fabergé branch in London had already been doing business for four years, thanks to royal patronage, and had the impressive pedigree of being the only branch outside the Russian Empire. Locally and globally, the stage was set for Fabergé's greatest British moment: an invitation to model animals from Edward VII and Queen Alexandra's beloved Sandringham estate in Norfolk.

Personal connections underpinned the story of the Sandringham animals and their international role. Fabergé himself was partly of Scandinavian descent, and his key patrons were the two Danish princesses Alexandra and Dagmar – Alix and Minny to their relatives – who became Queen Alexandra of Britain and Empress Maria Feodorovna of Russia. The two held on to their heritage and common family roots, while striving to ally their adopted nations in fashion and friendship. Spectacular gifts from the Fabergé workshops aided the sisterly enterprise of bringing Britain and Russia together.

This book, and the exhibition at the Sainsbury Centre it accompanies, explores the astonishing East Anglian saga, which placed the region in the middle of world affairs for a prolonged period. A path opened between the Winter Palace and Sandringham, a road from Russia to East Anglia – one intended to bring a better world, and even a new golden age. The dreams of international understanding plotted in the Norfolk idyll were ultimately blown apart by war and revolution. All that survives are Fabergé's magnificent animals, miniature testaments to the endurance of art.

FABERGÉ
Moss agate "painting" on gold easel *c.* 1910
Agate, silver, enamel
h. 140 mm
A LA VIEILLE RUSSIE, NEW YORK

FABERGÉ
Workmaster Victor Aarne
Framed photograph of Tsaritsa Maria Feodorovna *c.* 1890
Guilloché enamelled silver with borders of two-colour gold and half pearls; ivory back
h. 69 x w. 60 x d. 66 mm
ROYAL COLLECTION TRUST

FABERGÉ
Workmaster Victor Aarne
Framed photograph of Queen Alexandra *c.* 1907–1908
Two-colour gold, silver-gilt,
guilloché enamel, cabochon rubies,
mother-of-pearl, hand coloured photograph
h. 44 x w. 44 x d. 27 mm
ROYAL COLLECTION TRUST

CHAPTER ONE

Late-blooming Flowers

After the savage severity of a long Russian winter, the celebration of resurrection in an Orthodox Easter coincides with the promise of spring renewal. A melting in Lake Ladoga sends ice floes down the River Neva, to sweep through St Petersburg and past the windows of the Winter Palace as late as April. Then all is wild profusion as spring moves towards summer swelter and a procession of White Nights, when it never gets dark.

Given the brevity of the growing season across the Russian motherland, flowers have a special significance as tokens of love and devotion, marking weddings and funerals, being presented on birthdays and name-days, and brightening festivals – of which the greatest in the Orthodox calendar is Easter. They prompted many of Fabergé's finest works of art and showcased the genius of his workshops for evoking naturalism to an almost uncanny degree.

There is a reason, of course, why eggs are associated with Easter. The egg is a symbol of life set to burst forth in new and greater form. In Russia, as elsewhere, it is an ancient symbol. Of all Fabergé's output, the world is now most familiar with the fabulous saga of the 50 imperial eggs, of which 43 are known to survive. They began with a small egg of white enamel, opening to reveal a golden hen containing a bejewelled pendant, which Tsar Alexander III gave to his wife, Maria Feodorovna, for Easter 1885. It was based on an 18th-century egg she had known from her childhood in Denmark. He commissioned an egg for every successive Easter until his death in 1894. And then his son, Nicholas II, doubled the commission, with one egg for his wife, Alexandra Feodorovna, and another for his mother (except in 1904 and 1905, years of war and unrest, when production paused). They entailed spectacular feats of artistry and engineering and concealed stupendous surprises, playing to the recipient's affections. Maria Feodorovna loved nature, and birds in particular, and so her Easter gifts came to hold a floating swan, a strutting peacock spreading a rainbow tail, a singing bird of paradise and a clockwork cockerel crowing on the hour. This was art at its most sophisticated, masquerading as whimsy – as if the clever trinket had just fallen from a Christmas cracker.

Ingenuity was Fabergé's special hallmark. As he told the journal *Stolitsa i Usadba* (*Capital and Estate*), in 1914:

> *If you compare my things with those of such firms as Tiffany, Boucheron and Cartier, of course you will find the value of theirs is greater than mine. As far as they are concerned, it is possible to find a necklace in stock for one and a half million roubles. But of course these people are merchants and not artist-jewellers. Expensive things interest me little, if the value lies merely in the quantity of diamonds or pearls.*

In comparison with other jewellers supplying the royal court in St Petersburg, most notably Bolin and Kochli, the artful Fabergé had to accept prices that now seem surprisingly low. The *Basket of Flowers Egg* given to Empress Alexandra for Easter 1901, and now in the British Royal Collection, cost 6,850 roubles, compared with a record 212,244 roubles charged to the Romanovs for a Kochli sapphire parure. The most expensive egg was the *Mosaic Egg* of 1914, another of the three imperial eggs now in Britain's Royal Collection, billed at 28,300 roubles. Made for Empress Alexandra, it holds 5,300 tiny gemstones in a platinum setting, like coloured threads in a piece of embroidery, and opens to reveal a bejewelled stand with cameo portraits of the recipient's five children. Enamelled cameo-style images also decorated the *Catherine the Great Egg*, together with nearly 950 diamonds and 500 pearls, which was the Dowager Empress's Easter gift in that fateful year of 1914. She was so delighted with a work now in the

FABERGÉ
Basket of Flowers Egg 1901
Silver, parcel gilt, gold, oyster guilloché
and blue enamel, diamonds
h. 230 x w. 100 mm
ROYAL COLLECTION TRUST

1901

Hillwood Museum, Washington DC, that she wrote to her sister Alexandra at Sandringham: 'Fabergé is really the greatest genius of our age and I told him too: vous êtes un génie incomparable.'

The Danish sisters' background was far removed from the opulence and ostentation of the Russian court; their family lived in relatively straitened circumstances, and continued a Scandinavian restraint even when their father became Denmark's king. Empress Alexandra (Alicky), a princess from the German Grand Duchy of Hesse, had grown up with similar values. When her mother died, nursing the family through diphtheria, Alexandra came under the stern influence of her maternal grandmother, Queen Victoria. In her case, a chilly atmosphere would go beyond an inherited taste for unheated rooms. And amid thousands of servants, Alexandra and Nicholas (Nicky) tried to live like a bourgeois couple in corners of their palaces, though the fresh flowers the Empress craved were rushed from the French Riviera for sumptuous arrangements until the February Revolution ended Romanov rule in 1917.

But hopes were high with the new spring, and the new century, over Easter 1901. This came just weeks after Alicky's uncle, Edward VII, and Nicky's aunt, Alexandra, had been enthroned in England for their first State Opening of Parliament (a democratic institution forced upon the Romanovs, in the form of the Duma, by a revolution of 1905; but they never really accepted it). The Fabergé egg the Empress received that Easter played most fully to her love of contrived simplicity. Although hooped and latticed in gold and diamonds, an enamelled basket held the perfect likenesses of flowers that might have been picked from a Russian wood, meadow or cornfield. The bouquet of spring and summer blooms rising from a bed of golden moss included snowdrop, hellebore, narcissus, arum lily, cornflower, poppy, pansy, daisy, columbine, campanula, wild rose and jasmine, all set amid ears of corn and grasses. Here, wrought in gold and enamels, were flowers an empress could savour late in the season and, indeed, all year round.

The *Basket of Flowers Egg* was long disputed as an object of imperial provenance. The secrecy in which eggs were produced for the two empresses limited their documentation. Once delivered, they were kept in private apartments. But a Fabergé invoice dated 16 April 1901 recently came to light. The egg had also been spotted in a photograph from a 1902 charity exhibition held in St Petersburg under the patronage of Empress Alexandra – the only occasion in pre-revolutionary Russia when imperial eggs were shown in public. On the bottom shelf of a pyramid-shaped display cabinet, below the *Lilies of the Valley Egg* (1898) and the *Bouquet of Lilies Clock Egg* (1899), the *Basket of Flowers Egg* was clearly pictured. It differed significantly, however, from the egg being loaned to the Sainsbury Centre from the British Royal Collection in 2017. In the original version a masterly oyster enamelling, sparkling like the white and mother-of-pearl interior of the mollusc shell, covered the entire basket and base. Now its stand is enamelled in a visually less remarkable royal blue. But the turmoil of the 20th century may be perceived in that change.

Amid or after the revolutionary chaos of 1917, the *Basket of Flowers Egg* was presumably dropped and definitely damaged. First confiscated from the Anichkov Palace – Maria Feodorovna's home in St Petersburg – by the provisional authorities, the egg was taken to the Moscow Kremlin Armoury and valued at 15,000 roubles. Transferred to the government of the early Soviet republic, it was then sold for 2,000 roubles by the Antikvariat (the state-run organisation 'for the collection and conservation of treasures') in 1933 and exported.

The *Basket of Flowers Egg* entered the British Royal Collection in the year of its removal from Russia, with the buyer, Queen Mary, sharing the passion for Fabergé of her late mother-in-law, Queen Alexandra. At some point over the next 16 years, until the egg was reproduced in a 1949 book by Henry Charles Bainbridge – former manager of Fabergé's London branch – the broken base was re-enamelled. No invoice or any other record of the purchase, or information on how and when the damage was sustained or the repair effected, has so far been found. The mystery is now part of an astounding story of creativity and survival.

Imperial Easter Eggs were a year or more in the planning and making. So the *Basket of Flowers Egg* was being prepared when Fabergé represented Russia in the 1900 World's Fair in Paris. His display won a gold medal for work 'reaching the extreme limits of perfection' and 'transforming a jewel into a real objet d'art', as the citation put it. Shown alongside three imperial eggs there was a

FABERGÉ
Japanese Garden c. 1905
Nephrite, copper, rock crystal, enamel, rose diamonds, gold
h. 159 mm
A LA VIEILLE RUSSIE, NEW YORK

new line of botanical studies. Specimen plants of golden stalks, nephrite leaves and enamelled blooms and berries were set in hardstone pots or half-hollowed blocks of rock crystal cut and polished to give an impression of water in glass vases. As well as the gold medal, they carried off the compliment of instant imitation, as chief designer Franz P. Birbaum recalled:

> *When our enamelled flowers were first displayed at the Paris Exposition of 1900, they were immediately copied by German and Austrian manufacturers and the market was flooded with cheap versions – lacquers instead of enamels and glass instead of rock crystal in vases.*

None could ever outshine a Fabergé original; and today, after dozens of losses, the flower and fruit studies are nearly as rare as imperial eggs.

The art of mimicking nature is an exacting business. And the plant specimens that appeared to have been casually picked on a country walk were made in several painstaking stages. First, an artist worked with actual plants and botanical textbooks. Carl Fabergé then decided which designs went to the head workmaster – Mikhail Perkhin until 1903, then Henrik Wigström – and his team, to choose the method of manufacture and materials. Hardstones were then selected, latterly by head stone-cutter Peter Kremlev, and submitted in semi-rough form, first to Fabergé and then to the head workmaster, for final approval. Much of Russia's natural wealth lies in minerals – and in the lapidary production of Fabergé flowers, snow quartz could be fashioned into white petals, rhodonite into deep-pink blooms and berries, and turquoise into forget-me-nots. Nephrite, a type of Siberian jade, was superbly carved into thin leaves – curling, twisting, serrated, ridged and veined. Naturally occurring black spots within the green could suggest plant blight.

Cut stones went to the head workmaster for assembly and golden additions, and jewels were set by August Holmström and his son, Albert. Now pearls might become lily-of-the-valley flowers, in vogue as Tsaritsa Alexandra's favourites. Stems were crafted in alloys of gold – copper bringing hues of brown and red, silver a tinge of green. Texture was achieved by engraving and embossing; thorns were soldered and patinated. A flower's minutest details might comprise gold thread or a glint of rose-cut diamond or green demantoid garnet. Foliage was fixed to stalks with tiny gold pins or glue. And where stone and metal could not match the colour of nature, master enameller Nikolas Petrov (assisted by brother Dimitri) set to work in a demanding process to be described later in this book.

FABERGÉ
Daphne *c.* 1910
Gold, nephrite, enamel, diamonds, rock crystal
h. 112 mm
A LA VIEILLE RUSSIE, NEW YORK

Franz Birbaum held that inspiration for the flowers came when Fabergé was asked to repair a bunch of hardstone chrysanthemums from the palace of the Chinese emperor, which had been damaged during occupation by British and French forces in the Second Opium War. Beside an acknowledgement of Russian and European carving traditions, there were Japanese influences also. This is very clear in the *Pine Tree*, which is the only plant study known for certain to have been modelled from life with the Sandringham animals commission in 1907. But several other pieces in the British Royal Collection were possibly based on flora from the Norfolk estate. Dwarf bonsai trees were kept in a porch adjoining the plant house, and the Fabergé tribute has realistically carved gold bark, needles and cones set with diamonds. A pale-green bowenite pot is placed, Japanese-style, on a low table of aventurine quartz simulating wood. It was bought by the Prince of Wales (later George V) from Fabergé's London branch as a Christmas gift for Queen Alexandra in 1908.

The Sandringham estate Cottage Horticultural Society had staged its first show on 20 September 1866 with the aim to 'encourage labourers and others on the Royal Estate in the cultivation of their gardens and allotments, their wives and housekeepers in maintaining neatness and cleanliness in the cottages and the children in improving their needlework and writing', and with entertainment on the day from the 1st Norfolk Rifles. Successive annual shows were forerunners of the Sandringham Flower Show, now held on the last Wednesday in July. They were hugely popular attractions, with special excursion trains and coaches bringing visitors from near and far. Crowds were allowed to wander in the grounds – steadily remodelled with new lakes, rockery, flower beds, rose gardens and tree plantings and tended by more than a hundred gardeners in 1900. To 'prevent the intrusion of undesirable company', non-members paid a shilling for admission. Beside displays of cultivated flowers, fruit and

FABERGÉ
Workmaster Mikhail Perkhin
Box modelled as a potato *c.* 1890
Agate, gold fleur-de-lis
l. 95 x h. 64 x w. 57 mm
A LA VIEILLE RUSSIE, NEW YORK

vegetables, children competed with wildflower posies. Cut garden blooms included roses, carnations, lilies, pansies and sweet peas – most grown for scent as well as colour and all Fabergé favourites.

The genius of Fabergé was tested to the limit in a constant demand for gifts for every kind of royal celebration. He and his workmasters spent nine months of each year devising the novelties to please Queen Alexandra as presents on her birthday and Christmas tables – both in December. Birbaum called Alexandra Fabergé's 'greatest patroness' as well as the primary collector outside Russia of his flowers.

FABERGÉ
Pine Tree *c.* 1908
Bowenite, aventurine quartz, gold, brilliant diamonds
h. 123 x w. 62 x d. 58 mm
ROYAL COLLECTION TRUST

At one time 34 were owned by Grand Duchess Maria Pavlovna, sister-in-law of Maria Feodorovna and her rival as first lady of Russia, but 31 vanished in the revolution. Countess Mordvinova had a row of sculpted flowers in her marble bathroom; actress Elizabeth Balletta received several as gifts from Grand Duke Alexis (son of Alexander II); and prima ballerina Mathilda Kschessinska (mistress of two grand dukes) displayed some as table decorations at a dinner party on the eve of revolution. All these collections, along with those of two empresses, are now scattered and many are lost; today barely 80 flower and fruit studies are known to survive. Queen Alexandra's array of plant forms – 22 of the 26 now in the British Royal Collection – is the sole original assembly still intact. Gifts within the grouping include the holly sprig given by Alice Keppel, Edward VII's mistress, around the time that she presented the King with one of the most fabulous cigarette cases Fabergé ever produced.

FABERGÉ
Violet 1902
Gold, enamel, rock crystal
h. 114 mm
A LA VIEILLE RUSSIE, NEW YORK

An Imperial Presentation Gift, purchased in 1902 by Tsar Nicholas II and Alexandra Feodorovna, whose favourite colour was mauve.

CHAPTER TWO

In a Strange Land

On 23 March 1863 a royal train arrived at Wolferton Station in West Norfolk, on the newly opened branch line from King's Lynn to Hunstanton. Painted in claret livery, it was bringing Albert Edward, Prince of Wales, and his Danish bride, Alexandra (Alix to her family), back from honeymoon and on to their new base at Sandringham Hall. More than six decades later, in the dying days of 1925, similar transport bore the body of the much-loved Queen Dowager, 15 years the widow of Edward VII, for a state funeral and then for burial at Windsor.

Albert Edward – Bertie – was the eldest son and second of the nine children of Queen Victoria and Albert of Saxe-Coburg and Gotha, the Prince Consort. For the heir to the throne's 21st birthday, in 1862, his father had planned to give him his own country residence where he could provide a home for a future wife and family. At least 18 properties were considered across 13 counties, before Sandringham was chosen. Neighbouring Houghton Hall, the glorious Palladian mansion built from the 1720s for Sir Robert Walpole, Norfolk squire and Britain's first Prime Minister, and mothballed for nearly a century, was offered and rejected. It has been said that Prince Albert vetoed the purchase, shortly before he died in December 1861, on the grounds that it was too grand.

Sandringham Hall was an 18th-century white stucco house with a striking Victorian conservatory, set in what were quickly derided as 7,700 acres (3,100 hectares) of sand. As Lady Macclesfield, the Princess's Lady-of-the-Bedchamber, complained:

> *There are numerous coverts but no fine woods, large unenclosed turnip fields, with an occasional haystack to break the line of the horizon. It would be difficult to find a more ugly or desolate-looking place, and there is no neighbourhood or any other countervailing advantage. The wind blows keen from the Wash and the Spring is said to be unendurable in that part of Norfolk . . . As there was all England wherein to choose I do wish they had had a finer house in a more picturesque and cheerful situation.*

But the windswept landscape close to the North Sea reminded Alix of her native Denmark, and beyond the park those numerous coverts, plus heaths and fields, promised fine hunting and shooting for a prince embarking on what would prove to be nearly four decades of enforced leisure, with no expense spared. So Sandringham was bought for £220,000 from Charles Spencer Cowper, stepson of Viscount Palmerston, the then Prime Minister. The estate would be steadily improved and extended to the 20,000 acres (8,000 hectares) it occupies today, spreading over seven villages and 13 parishes. By the time Albert Edward came to the throne, as Edward VII, in 1901, all that remained of the old house was the Victorian conservatory, by then a billiard room beside a bowling alley. A vast new Jacobean-style pile, designed by A.J. Humbert and extending to 365 rooms at its peak (scores were removed later), was both a royal retreat and a centre of stately entertainment. When in London, the Prince and Princess of Wales held court at Marlborough House and, during Victoria's long withdrawal as 'the widow of Windsor', were the visible centre of British monarchy – Alix becoming far and away the royal family's most popular member. But Sandringham was vital to the couple from the outset. And while Bertie would be a guest at countless house-parties – and shooting parties – all over the country, as well as enjoying many tours and cures abroad, the Norfolk estate was the prime setting for extended family gatherings, involving many of the crowned heads of Europe. For Alix it became first a nursery and then a menagerie, and finally a paradise of near-complete seclusion that she couldn't bear to leave.

Queen Victoria's claim to the British throne came through the Hanoverian line; her mother was German also. She wed a German prince, and four of their five daughters were betrothed to other German princes – starting with the eldest, Vicky, who at 17 was married to Frederick (Fritz), the Crown Prince of Prussia. With a strong intellect matched by a sense of family purpose, she bore on teenage shoulders the mighty task of

FABERGÉ
Workmaster Henrik Wigström
Box with a view of Sandringham House 1908–1910
Nephrite, two-colour gold, half pearls, sepia enamel
h. 32 x w. 103 x d. 76 mm
ROYAL COLLECTION TRUST

liberalising the advancing military power of Prussia. But for starters, Vicky – in cahoots with her newly widowed mother – arranged Bertie's marriage to Alix. It was all done in a rush after what Victoria called Bertie's 'Fall'. A youthful indiscretion – the first of many flings – would for ever be blamed by the moralistic matriarch for the premature death of her adored husband. But Albert was really killed by overwork, Victorian medical standards and the strain of living with the imperious and neurotic Queen Victoria. Since no suitable German princesses were available to keep Bertie on the straight and narrow, the matchmakers looked northwards to Denmark.

The London Protocol of 1852 had awarded the disputed duchies of Schleswig and Holstein to Denmark and appointed the impoverished Prince Christian of Schleswig-Holstein-Sonderburg-Glücksburg as heir to the childless Danish king. Christian and his wife Louise raised their six children comparatively modestly in Copenhagen, but with the highest of ambitions to advance through royal connections. The two eldest sons became kings of Denmark and Greece; the third declined the thrones of Norway and Bulgaria. The two eldest daughters, strikingly beautiful and with skilful parental promotion as models of Victorian virtue, changed the world. Alexandra and Dagmar – Alix and Minny – were both in the sights of Tsar Alexander II of Russia as a possible bride for his son and heir. Victoria and Vicky got in first, by bagging 'sweet Alix' for Bertie. Such was the completeness of their plan that the bridegroom – while obligingly declaring that he had fallen deeply in love – was allowed to invite only four friends to a crowded wedding at St George's Chapel, Windsor. While the couple were exchanging their vows, a four-year-old Prussian prince in Highland dress had a tantrum and threw his toy dirk into the aisle. This was the first public appearance in Britain of the future Kaiser Wilhelm II.

FABERGÉ
Workmaster Henrik Wigström
Framed view of Sandringham House, 1908
Nephrite, gold, half pearls, sepia enamel, ivory
h. 90 x w. 152 x d. 71 mm
ROYAL COLLECTION TRUST

Enamel scenes like this were painted in warm sepia tones on engine-turned metal panels. They were then fired with powdered glass and polished to reflect the light when held in the hands.

FABERGÉ
Workmaster Mikhail Perkhin
Five-colour gold double marriage cup before 1896
Gold
h. 92 mm
A LA VIEILLE RUSSIE, NEW YORK

This gorgeous miniature tower parts in the middle to form two identical vessels – a double marriage cup. Each golden triangle and rectangle is textured in fine feathering and bears a peacock's eye. In Russian folklore the peacock symbolises love, marriage and motherhood – as well as spring, the sun and immortality.

Confessing to Lord Palmerston that the sight of any happy couple 'plunges daggers into the Queen's widowed heart', Victoria was further upset that this particular pair corresponded in English. To the British monarch, the language of intimacy was German, and Alix was also warned not to make Bertie politically pro-Danish in any manner of speaking. Family tensions worsened after Alix's father became King Christian IX of Denmark in November 1863, and the crisis over Schleswig (populated by Danes) and Holstein (predominantly German) deepened into armed conflict. The following April, Prussia crushed Denmark and occupied the contested duchies, with Fritz, Bertie's brother-in-law, at the head of the victorious army. It was the first of the wars through which the Prussians would enforce, by 1871, their dominance within a united Germany. And it ensured that Alix and Minny, so firm in their affections and in the opposite opinions also, were anti-German ever after.

The world stage was set for the sisters to assume leading roles when, in November 1866, Minny married the Russian Tsarevich, the future Alexander III (Sasha to his family), and became Grand Duchess Maria Feodorovna. Her departure from Denmark prompted this Hans Christian Andersen poem:

Farewell, Princess Dagmar, as you
leave for greatness and glory,
an Imperial Crown will sprout
from your bridal garland;
May God let his sunshine glow
in you and your new home,
and may every tear, which your
parting induces, turn into a pearl!

Minny had previously been engaged to Sasha's older brother, who had died of meningitis. At the time of the wedding the Russian Empire stretched from Finland and Poland to Alaska and covered one-sixth of the planet. It was exceeded in scale only by the British Empire, which spread across a quarter of the globe, from Canada to Australasia, and on which the sun so famously never set. The 'British' Raj alone ran from Yemen to Singapore and included most of the modern-day countries of India, Pakistan, Bangladesh and Myanmar. Diminished Denmark had just concluded a most dramatic dynastic coup. The two brides, close confidantes who had shared a bedroom until Alix turned 16, were now determined to bring Britain and Russia together against Germany; and the strength of prevailing Anglo-German ties was not the only obstacle to their unpromising project. Barely ten years after the Crimean War, and with ongoing rivalry further east, Britain and Russia remained hostile powers. Undaunted, Alix and Minny were prepared to work over decades to stress similarities and shared cultural interests in particular. In the early years they caused a sensation when appearing together, in London and St Petersburg, wearing identical outfits. In August 1873 the *Illustrated London News* published a print of their carriage ride in Hyde Park, with matching costumes and lapdogs. With an actual age difference of three years, the sisters contrived to look like twins. The we-two-are-one political message behind their fashion statement was all too clear.

While the royal families of 19th-century Europe veered wildly between war and peace, Victoria had a more consistent hostility towards her eldest son. She poured vitriol into journals and letters, deeming Bertie to be 'totally totally unfit' for the grave business of kingship; such opprobrium was lightened chiefly by outbreaks of sentimental pity. Bertie had appalled his parents from childhood by rebelling against a regime of rigorous study, and now he was apparently lost to pleasure: smoking, drinking, gluttony, gambling, hunting, shooting, fast company, gossip, practical jokes and rough-and-tumble horseplay. Alix shared her husband's taste for the first and last of these, and she further ignored Victoria's pleas to give up hunting (while frequently voicing the hope that 'the poor fox' would escape). Increasingly and often very conveniently deaf, she also tried to turn a blind eye to Bertie's affairs, despite the recurrent threat – and occasional reality – of scandal.

The great power that was Queen Victoria pursued a policy of isolation towards her eldest son. Readily sharing official papers with Tory opposition leaders, she vetoed any consultative role for her frivolous heir, who was thought incapable of keeping a secret. Indeed, she long seemed to assume that monarchy itself would die with her, so absolute was Bertie's unsuitability to succeed. Victoria paid a first visit to Sandringham as late as 1871 – summoned by news that her errant son was perilously ill with typhoid. His recovery when on the brink of death, celebrated in a thanksgiving service at St Paul's Cathedral, rescued Victoria from a decade of deepening unpopularity. But a restoration of health brought a return of maternal disapproval. She came again to Sandringham briefly in 1889, then called no more.

Engraving of Princesses Alexandra and Dagmar by William Biscombe Gardner for the *Illustrated London News* in July 1873.

PRIVATE COLLECTION, SUFFOLK

Like their own parents, Alix and Minny both had six children. Each lost a son in infancy, and later their favourite son at the age of 28 – Prince Albert Victor, the Duke of Clarence and Avondale, who was Alix and Bertie's eldest child, dying of influenza at Sandringham in 1892. As they entered middle age, the sisters retained their youthful beauty. Indeed, almost to the end of their lives (both died at 80), they could look un-aged – and younger than their daughters. Frequently drawn and painted, they were the darlings of portrait photography via hundreds and thousands of radiant images (much like Diana Spencer, a future Princess of Wales, born on the Sandringham estate in 1961). The 19th-century Princess of Wales was ostensibly a rather powerless figure within a constitutional monarchy and developing democracy. But Russia was avowedly autocratic, though power had been held in male hands since the death of Catherine the Great in 1796. And when in March 1881 Alexander II was torn apart by a bomb, having freed the serfs and espoused limited liberal reform, the Romanovs were fatefully – fatally – returned to absolutist rule. The constant threat of assassination lent further distance, and henceforth Alix was haunted by the danger to 'darling little Minny'. The new Tsar and Tsaritsa had a famously happy marriage – it was said of the bear-like Alexander III, for whom trials of strength were both a party piece and a demonstration of power, that the two things he wished never to break were the peace of Europe and the Seventh Commandment – and his wife was steadily at his side. At 33, Minny knew all about the mystique of spectacle: as Maria Feodorovna, she looked the image of an empress in bejewelled finery, on carefully staged public appearances.

Alix was the more soft-hearted of the sisters; her kindness and gentleness commanded love as well as loyalty.

Dagmar and Alix: the double act, 1873

DAVID WILLIAM CRIPPS COLLECTION

Maria Feodorovna and Alexander III with their children (left to right: Michael, Nicholas, Olga, Xenia and George) in 1888.

DAVID WILLIAM CRIPPS COLLECTION.

While the Prince of Wales was unpopular with some of his Norfolk tenants, amid strict enforcement of the needs of a shooting estate above all others, his wife was beyond reproach. She emerged with celestial credit even from a diatribe published as *Eighteen Years on the Sandringham Estate* by 'the Lady Farmer'. After a torrent of disgruntlement, Louise Creswell added:

> *It never occurs to me that the Princess is a woman at all but some exquisite little being wafted straight from fairyland to say and do the kindest and prettiest things all her life and never, never grow old or ugly.*

In the summer of 1881 a tombstone was placed in London's Brompton Cemetery. It read: 'In memory of Elizabeth Jones. Who died May 13th 1881. For 14 years the faithful servant of Alexandra, Princess of Wales, by whom this monument is erected.' Mrs Jones – Johnnie – had assisted Alix through illness and childbirth, and the Princess in turn paid nightly vigil at her attendant's deathbed. But less than a month later Alix was grieving again, and commissioning a memorial stone for the grounds of Marlborough House for the latest object of her devotion. It bore the inscription: 'Bonny. Favourite rabbit of HRH the Princess of Wales. Died June 8 1881.' In time the tribute to Bonny the bunny would be joined by seven canine grave-markers, with a larger pack of pet memorials at Sandringham.

More and more, after Bertie and the children, and then the grandchildren, animals claimed the Princess's affections. Although the word 'favourite' recurred on memorials to faithful beastly companions, whose lifespans generally run so sadly short of ours, Alix doted on dozens of dogs at any one time. Her love of canine kind was one of those 'sweet' traits that brought her close to Victoria – and it was reflected in gifts of portraits of beloved mutts by the Great Yarmouth-raised artist Charles Burton Barber, which still hang in Sandringham. A Burton Barber likeness of Beattie, painted for the Prince of Wales, shows a Pomeranian descended from Arctic hunting dogs lying on a tiger-skin (28 such kingly beasts had been despatched by Bertie in a single hunt during his 1875-6 Indian tour; then again, he had felled the same number of flamingos with one blast from a punt gun on a Nile cruise in 1869). A tombstone in the pets' cemetery near the kennels reads: 'Beattie, for 10 years the faithful companion of HRH the Prince of Wales; died at Sandringham, Jan. 13 1893.'

FABERGÉ
Group of Rabbits *c.* 1907
Agate, rose diamonds
h. 46 x w. 84 x d. 67 mm
ROYAL COLLECTION TRUST

FABERGÉ
Brown Bear *c.* 1907
Agate, rose diamonds
h. 25 x w. 39 x d. 17 mm
ROYAL COLLECTION TRUST

At one time Sandringham had a zoo, with a pair of bears named Charlie and Polly – souvenirs of Bertie's 1875-6 tour of India, which were eventually relocated to London Zoo. Visiting Sandringham in 1887, Charles Dickens Jr. wrote in the *All the Year Round* journal that his father had founded:

'There is a bear-pit with a pair of shaggy bears; the biggest shows a wonderful alacrity in climbing, and will yield to no bear, not even to the bears of Berne, in his powers of catching.'

It seems that this Fabergé model was less a friendly symbol of Russia than a fond reminder of a formidable animal that Sandringham had lost. But, alas, bears were still known in Edwardian Norfolk in fairs and circuses and, chained and muzzled, 'dancing' to musical accompaniment as street entertainment.

William Nicholson
1872–1949
Queen Victoria 1899
Chromolithograph print
h. 571 x w. 419 x d. 40 mm
VICTORIA AND ALBERT MUSEUM

Victoria's preference for pets in abundance was shared by her offspring and wider family. One of the earliest of royal-family home movies captures a visit by the Romanovs to Balmoral in 1896. Jerky and flickering images contrast courtly constraint with beastly exuberance. While the visitors, Tsar Nicholas and Empress Alexandra, Minny's son and daughter-in-law, trot dutifully alongside the carriage bearing the elderly Queen around the garden, there is a corresponding chaos – and doubtless a cacophony – of dogs. William Nicholson's pared-down portrait print of the formidable monarch in 1899 is essentially how history has remembered her. Much detail was omitted, but the Queen's mournful black outfit was accessorised by a perky Skye terrier at her shrouded heels.

Queen Victoria and her grandson, Kaiser Wilhelm II, shared a passion for dachshunds. Alexandra's love of all dog breeds included even this canine symbol of the Germany she otherwise detested.

FABERGÉ
Dachshund *c.* 1907
Agate, rose diamonds
h. 43 x w. 73 x d. 21 mm
ROYAL COLLECTION TRUST

CHAPTER THREE

An Enigmatic Nature

At the Pan-Russian Exhibition held in Moscow in 1882, a jeweller called Fabergé caused a sensation with replicas of the fourth-century BC Scythian Treasure unearthed in Crimea in 1867 and displayed in the Hermitage Museum. He won a gold medal and a tribute from Tsar Alexander III, who declared his copy indistinguishable from the original. Maria Feodorovna bought her husband a pair of cufflinks, and it was agreed that objects made by the House of Fabergé should be shown in the Hermitage as splendid examples of contemporary Russian craftsmanship.

Peter Carl Fabergé (1846–1920) had been born in St Petersburg, but his father, Gustav Fabergé, was of Huguenot and Baltic German descent, and – significantly and perhaps crucially – his mother, Charlotte Jungstedt, had Swedish or Danish ancestry. His father was a goldsmith with a modest jewellery business, but in 1860 Gustav moved the family temporarily to Dresden, where the boy (who preferred to be known as Carl, although back in Russia it would be Karl Gustavovich) was introduced to sublime collections of historical jewellery in the Green Vaults.

For three years from 1861 Carl explored the continent, in what was more of a great apprenticeship than a Grand Tour, as he received tuition from respected goldsmiths in Germany, France and England, savoured Italian *pietra dura* art treasures in highly polished coloured stones, toured many renowned museums and galleries across Europe, and attended a commercial college in Paris. In 1864 the Fabergés returned to St Petersburg and Carl joined the family firm. Two years later Gustav started to supply the Imperial Cabinet, helping Carl the following year to begin a decade of voluntary work at the Hermitage Museum, reassembling antiquities and appraising metalwork and jewellery acquisitions. The Hermitage was then housed in part of the Winter Palace, and a young man of high ambition could scarcely have been closer to power and patronage. In 1875 Carl took over Gustav's business and married his cousin, Augusta Jakobs. Three sons who survived to adulthood – Eugene, Agathon and Alexander – would be born over a four-year period from 1874, with a fourth, Nicholas, following a decade later. All joined the clan company, which, until his premature death in 1895, also included Carl's designer brother (the original Agathon).

Alfred Lyndhurst Pocock (1881–1962)
Portrait of Carl Fabergé
Plaster
h. 159 x w. 121 mm
A LA VIEILLE RUSSIE, NEW YORK

Alfred Lyndhurst Pocock was chosen by Fabergé's London branch to model animals in wax for Queen Alexandra in 1905 when a Royal Academy Schools student. His close links with the company for the next decade are demonstrated by this unique relief plaster portrait.

Once he had caught the eye of the Tsar, and still more the Danish-born Empress, Carl was swift to capitalise on a key connection. In 1885 he was appointed court supplier, and Alexander III commissioned the first Imperial Easter Egg as a present for his wife, with ever more fabulous enamelled and bejewelled oval forms ensuing until an abrupt halt in 1917. But in this unparalleled operation even the least impressive piece on offer was a unique work of art, which, furthermore, appeared to have been conceived and produced by a single maker.

FABERGÉ
Workmaster Henrik Wigström
Miniature by Vasili Zuiev
Imperial column 1909
Gold, diamonds
h. 108 mm
A LA VIEILLE RUSSIE, NEW YORK

A red and green gold column in the Louis XVI style, decorated with laurel and acanthus leaves, surmounted by the Russian Imperial Eagle. The suspended miniature portrait of Tsar Nicholas II, by Vasili Zuiev (active 1908-17), is topped by an Imperial Crown and set with diamonds.

The Tsar awarded this impressive work to German courtier August Ludwig Count zu Eulenburg in June 1909.

FABERGÉ
Cigarette case 1908
Two-colour gold, guilloché enamel,
brilliant and rose-cut diamonds
h. 17 x w. 96 x d. 70 mm
ROYAL COLLECTION TRUST

FABERGÉ
Workmaster August Holmström
Cigarette case *c.* 1898
Enamel, diamonds
l. 95 mm
A LA VIEILLE RUSSIE, NEW YORK

A cigarette case in sunburst yellow enamel with diamond Imperial Crown, awarded by Tsaritsa Alexandra Feodorovna to an Austrian colonel in 1899.

The Art Nouveau decoration of this gold and royal blue enamel cigarette case has an Egyptian-inspired design of gold ginkgo leaves with rose diamond buds.

FABERGÉ
Cigarette case *c.* 1910
Gold, enamel, rose diamonds
A LA VIEILLE RUSSIE, NEW YORK
l. 92 mm

The last decades of imperial Russia required a staggering amount of gifts. The royal family sustained cohesion and authority by bestowing tokens of affection, esteem and appreciation; the adroit among the aspirant classes and organisations hoping to curry favour with the reigning power sought to draw attention to themselves by means more subtle than bribery. Fabergé himself recognised this when, interviewed in 1914, he said his wares suited occasions when 'it is awkward to give expensive jewels'. Then there were the necessary gifts of diplomatic exchange by which Russia might raise its profile and foster friendship abroad. All these needs were met in the Fabergé workshops. Here the significance of small things lay in the production of a brilliant paradox: a supreme excellence that might also be taken rather lightly (small wonder that some would ultimately dismiss these masterly little artworks as trivia, even as kitsch). As Henry Bainbridge recalled:

It was all those beautiful articles of fantaisie, those bibelots for the table, which made his fame all the world over . . . stick – and parasol-handles, electric-bell pushes, match boxes, pencils, clocks, frames, paper knives, cigarette lighters, cigarette boxes, bonbonnieres, necessaires and his flowers and animals, on all these he simply let himself go and used not only gold, silver, enamel and precious stones, but all the Siberian semi-precious stones, jade or nephrite, orletz, rock crystal and many more.

Beyond the grand stores in St Petersburg, Moscow, Kiev and Odessa, the latest miniature masterpieces were showcased in a London outlet that was more a courtly and celebrity salon than a mere shop. Opening in 1903 in Berners Hotel, it moved first to a room in Portman House and then to premises in Dover Street, before a final incarnation in a formal store in New Bond Street. Anonymity was respected and an air of secrecy prevailed

FABERGÉ
Poppy and clematis flower cigarette cases in the Art Nouveau style *c.* 1900
Silver and gem-set silver
l. 107 and 92 mm
ANDRE RUZHNIKOV

FABERGÉ
Workmaster Julius Rappoport
Dessert Set *c.* 1890
Silver, copper, gold
Knives: l. 203 mm; forks: l. 197 mm
A LA VIEILLE RUSSIE, NEW YORK

This set of fruit and cheese cutlery illustrates Fabergé's fondness for japonisme and fusion of excellence.

Handles have been repurposed from a traditional Japanese utility knife called a kogatana. Most are signed by master craftsmen, such as Ishiguro Masaharu, Nakajima Toshiharu and Hamano Masayuki. Each handle is uniquely ornamented with Japanese motifs.

Metalwork techniques include shibuichi, an alloy of silver and copper blended in varied proportions to achieve colours ranging from grey to blue or green. Others are made of copper, and some are shakudo, an alloy of gold and copper treated to resemble lacquer.

– as if the giving of such gorgeous tokens was not only intimate, but perhaps also illicit. As Mrs Keppel's daughter, Violet Trefusis, wrote to her lover Vita Sackville-West in 1918, gifts such as stockings, chocolates and flowers signified 'slight flirtation', whereas cigarette cases, lingerie and 'Fabergé trifles' were suggestive of a relationship 'in danger of becoming serious'. In this light, the Fabergé cigarette case that Violet's mother gave to the King a decade earlier is heavily symbolic: as well as the diamond tail-biting snake emblem of undying devotion, the moiré-effect guilloché enamel is reminiscent of lingerie silk. And beside the constant Fabergé concern for customer seduction with newness and novelty, there was a ceaseless adherence to the bottom line. Lovely little things had to be made affordable – and Fabergé privately complained that royal clients drove the hardest bargain of all.

Affordability is a relative term, of course. Although rapidly industrialising late 19th-century Russia was gaining a middle class, levels of rural and urban poverty remained inconceivable to 21st-century eyes. However ugly the world around him, Carl Fabergé strove for the creation of beauty. Criticised for the conservatism of his early designs, based on 18th-century France and European neoclassicism, his execution was always exemplary and his business model increasingly enlightened. He introduced a house doctor, a canteen and electric light. As his enterprise grew, he came to make nothing with his own hands, but remained the overall authority on design, quality control, finance and marketing. By 1900, 300 goldsmiths, jewellers, enamellers and stone-carvers, creating thousands of diverse objects each year, were gathered under the same roof as his grand, vitrine-lined shop at 24 Bolshaya Morskaya. Here, too, specialists made immaculate presentation boxes (usually in holly wood lined with cream satin and velvet). Under this big umbrella, workmasters effectively ran small firms, with their own craftsmen and apprentices. On special objects the workmasters were allowed to add their initials alongside the company stamp. Such stellar artists were often Scandinavian.

While Carl Fabergé's design ideas to please the nobles and royals of St Petersburg came to be influenced by Japan and China as well as Europe, the Moscow shop and silver workshops he opened in 1887, behind the Bolshoi Theatre, aimed at an emerging clientele of merchants. Often decorated in rich and jewelled colours of cloisonné enamel, the resulting objects harked back to old Russian folk tales – especially to legends of medieval warriors – and played to a new national sentiment. Ironically the enterprise was headed by Englishman Allan Bowe, who had been born in South Africa. Until their partnership ended acrimoniously in 1906, the man who enjoyed family summer holidays at Cromer, so close to Sandringham, may have been the business brains of the Fabergé empire. He also oversaw a celebration of more contemporary militarism from the Moscow branch. The Fabergé link to Russia's military machine produced trophies for army and naval officers, before it finally exploded with fatal consequences for all that had gone before. And Allan Bowe, who retained substantial business interests in Russia after breaking with Fabergé, lost the lot in 1917. He ended up living in a Clacton-on-Sea bungalow called The Dacha.

Skill was of paramount importance in every element of Fabergé's production, but perhaps his greatest claim to fame – an element to be admired in the most extravagant imperial egg and the most delicate flower study – is his revival of the art of enamelling. And most notable of all is the elevation of guilloché enamelling, across 145 ensuing shades, to a standard that cannot be matched today. On a metal base – typically gold, platinum or silver-gilt – engine-turned patterns would be incised as if on a printing plate. The effect might be of sunburst rays, marine waves or the ripples of moiré silk; the enamelled carriage of a *Sedan Chair*, lately with A La Vieille Russie in New York (a family firm established in Kiev in 1851, and relocating to Paris after the revolution), is patterned with rose-entwined trellising. Over such a grooved ground a layer of powdered glass is then fired in a kiln to produce enamel. Once the piece has cooled, the mottled enamel surface must be pumiced to make it shine and searched for the smallest imperfections. The layering and firing process is then repeated many times for translucence – with an inner-glow as if light itself has been trapped in the glassy depths. Each firing carries a risk of cracking, and therefore of the process having to begin again from scratch. Fabergé's reported failure rate of less than one-third of pieces undergoing guilloché enamelling is itself a remarkable statistic. The pursuit of perfection can prove far more costly than that.

Feodor Rückert
1840–1917
Cup and cover *c.* 1890
Silver-gilt and enamel
h. 342 mm
THE ROSALINDE AND ARTHUR GILBERT COLLECTION
ON LOAN TO THE VICTORIA AND ALBERT MUSEUM

Feodor Ivanovich Rückert was the supreme master of cloisonné enamelling in the Russian style, though actually of German origin and born Friedrich Mauritz Rückert. The silver and goldsmith opened a workshop in Moscow in 1886, and swiftly contracted to sell most of his brilliantly decorated objects through Fabergé. Glass paste was painted into designs on metal vessels traced in pools edged in metal wires, before repeated painting and firing and final gilding. His popular themes were Russian history and folklore.

FABERGÉ
HMS Talbot Kovsh *c.* 1904
Silver
h. 390 x w. 360 x l. 550 mm
THE TRUSTEES OF THE ROYAL NAVY TROPHY FUND

A Kovsh was a wooden drinking vessel or ladle from medieval Russia, shaped like a Viking longboat or a water bird. Its revival in Fabergé's Moscow silverworks, with folk-hero figureheads, played to traditional and patriotic tastes of the Russian merchant classes at the turn of the 20th century.

This typically fearsome example was presented by Tsar Nicholas II to the officers' mess of HMS Talbot, the British cruiser that rescued wounded sailors from the Battle of Chemulpo Bay, at the start of the Russo-Japanese War. The 1904-5 conflict began and ended in Russian defeats.

FABERGÉ
Imperial Trophy 1900
Silver
h. 370 mm
Andre Ruzhnikov

Trophy presented by Empress Alexandra Feodorovna.

FABERGÉ
Pear Blossom c. 1904
Rock crystal, gold, enamel, nephrite, diamonds, with original holly wood and silver box
h. 160 x w. 100 x d. 70 mm
THE QUEEN'S OWN WARWICKSHIRE AND WORCESTERSHIRE YEOMANRY REGIMENTAL CHARITABLE TRUST

In 1905 the Countess of Dudley presented this treasure to The Queen's Own Worcestershire Hussars to mark 1900-03 service in South Africa, in and after the Boer War. The Pear Blossom is depicted on the Regimental Badge, and the Fabergé bloom continues to feature in Armistice Day events and other regimental occasions in Worcestershire. The Countess of Dudley was born Rachel Gurney, from the Norfolk banking family.

FABERGÉ
Workmaster Henrik Wigström
Rothschild Sedan chair 1910
Gold, enamel, rock crystal, mother-of-pearl
h. 76 x w. 41 x l. 108 mm
A LA VIEILLE RUSSIE, NEW YORK

Sedan chair in the Louis XV style, made for Baron Leopold de Rothschild.

FABERGÉ
Photograph frame
Gold, rubies, pearls, enamel
h. 120 x w. 85 mm
PRIVATE COLLECTION, NORFOLK

Fabergé completed many commissions for the Rothschild family. This frame contains a portrait of Aline de Rothschild, who married the politician and businessman Sir Edward Sassoon.

CHAPTER FOUR

After the Fair

Across the arts in the Victorian period, nature became the major vehicle for innovation and expression. The natural world gave successive movements – Pre-Raphaelitism, Impressionism, the Arts and Crafts Movement and Art Nouveau – their core themes, and came to provide art that was now, and most importantly, progressive, with its essential identity. Deeply affected by the arts around him, Carl Fabergé embraced natural form as a principal means of expression. The 1907 Sandringham commission played to his project of exploring the animal kingdom with an unfettered sense of adventure. Fascinatingly, this work was destined to live in one of the most complex and unspoiled natural regions in northern Europe: East Anglia.

East Anglia had been the richest part of England in the Middle Ages – hence the unparalleled legacy of medieval churches – but its wealth had been lost with the collapse of the wool economy by the early 17th century. By the late 19th century the rural eastern counties, hit by further agricultural decline spurred by poor harvests and cheap New World grain imports from the 1870s, were among the poorest in the land. Fishing, trapping and shooting were vital to the rural household economy – with poaching endemic across the countryside, despite severe punishments including, until 1868, transportation to Australia. Influenced by naturalistic French painting, photographer Peter Henry Emerson showed the hardship of rural labour in his first album, *Life and Landscape on the Norfolk Broads*, in 1886. The most celebrated image, *Gathering Water-Lilies*, appeared to show a scene of languid romance. In fact the couple in the rowing boat, a father and daughter, are harvesting flowers to bait a

Peter Henry Emerson
Gathering Water-Lilies 1887
From *Life and Landscape on the Norfolk Broads*, Plate IX
NORFOLK COUNTY COUNCIL LIBRARY AND INFORMATION SERVICE

Gunton Hall, Norfolk 1865
Engraving in the *Illustrated London News* marking a visit by the Prince and Princess of Wales
PRIVATE COLLECTION.

bow-net at the back of the vessel. It will be used to catch tench for the family table.

Norfolk had been the cradle of the national agricultural workers' union. In January 1906 the Liberals swept East Anglia in a General Election landslide, pledging to found a welfare state. In July a conference in North Walsham's Angel Hotel established the Eastern Counties Labourers & Small Holders Union – renamed the National Agricultural Labourers & Rural Workers Union four years later. Founding secretary George Edwards, born at Marsham, near Aylsham, had missed school entirely, having worked as a crow-scarer from the age of six. After his wife taught him to read and write he was eventually returned as a Labour MP for South Norfolk.

Into the 19th and 20th centuries generally impoverished East Anglia retained a patchwork of sometimes enormous feudal estates, some of which – most notably the seat of the Coke-family, Earls of Leicester, on the north Norfolk coast at Holkham – had been models of agricultural efficiency and innovation. But for their owners, hunting and shooting could be at least as important as the farming that underwrote the sporting operation, and such rights were zealously policed.

The Prince and Princess of Wales were active figures in their adopted county, with many rounds of official engagements to found schools and hospitals, launch shows and receive military presentations. But the *Norfolk Chronicle* was most likely to report the presence of the Prince in the winter months – he would invariably be at Sandringham for his birthday (9 November) and that of Alix (1 December), and also for a family Christmas. Such celebrations were handily timed and placed for a keen country sportsman who, with or without his wife, would go on to stay with Earl and Countess Leicester at Holkham, Lord and Lady Walsingham at Merton Hall near Thetford, or Lord and Lady Hastings at Melton Constable Hall near Holt, for visits in which three-day shoots usually led the entertainments laid on for the royal house-party. The haul of game was generally prodigious. Of one 11-day gathering at Holkham over New Year 1866, the *Norfolk Chronicle* reported:

> *So considerable was the destruction of hares, rabbits, pheasants, &c., during the Royal visit that on one day 2 tons 19 cwt. of game were forwarded from Wells Station to Leadenhall Market.*

The cost to the host could be colossal, and none paid more than the 5th Baron Suffield, whose Gunton Hall near Cromer, a Palladian mansion greatly extended by Samuel Wyatt in the late 18th century and now complete with its own railway station, was a magnet for the Prince of Wales – latterly with mistress Lillie Langtry lodged close by at Elderton Lodge. In December 1882, on the eve of yet another royal visit, the mansion all but burned down. Local rumour whispered that Lord Suffield had ordered the deterrent of a little fire in the vicinity of the royal apartment, which had then raged out of control.

Bertie, and more occasionally Alix, enjoyed the attractions of Elveden Hall, on the estate bought by Edward Cecil Guinness, 1st Earl of Iveagh, in 1894. The brewing heir revived the sumptuous hospitality and sporting tradition established under former owner Maharajah Duleep Singh, with winter house-parties for royal and aristocratic guests. King Edward was shooting there in January 1910, four months before his death.

Bertie and Alix were also winter guests of William Tyssen-Amherst, who served as a Norfolk Tory MP for 12 years before becoming Baron Amherst of Hackney in 1892. Didlington Hall, his sprawling Italianate mansion on a 7,000-acre (2,800-hectare) estate near Swaffham, was one of the great treasure houses of England, with fine furniture and finest library. Big clues to the connoisseur owner's chief interest came via seven gigantic stone carvings of lion-headed and human-bodied goddesses lined in front of the East Wing – ferocious figures whose potential for violence had once inspired fervent acts of appeasement. Carved in the 14th century BC for the Karnak temple complex in the Nile Valley at Thebes, the Sahkmet sculptures led to a gallery containing other ancient Egyptian antiquities. Alix and Bertie were happily reminded of their 1869 Nile cruise. The private museum also inspired a Swaffham lad called Howard Carter, whose archaeological explorations in Egypt would culminate in the 1922 discovery of Tutankhamun's tomb. But Didlington shooting parties ceased when Lord Amherst found he had paid dearly for concentrating on his life as a politician, host and collector. He had left the running of his estate to a land agent who had robbed and ruined him to fund a gambling habit, and who committed suicide in 1906. To meet enormous debts, the treasure house was dismantled – library sales drawing global interest, with 16 Caxton volumes bought by John Pierpont Morgan in New York for $500,000. Lord Amherst died soon afterwards and then the estate was sold; the hall was demolished in 1952. Those ancient Egyptian goddesses now guard New York's Metropolitan Museum of Art.

Egyptian sculptures at Didlington Hall
PRIVATE COLLECTION

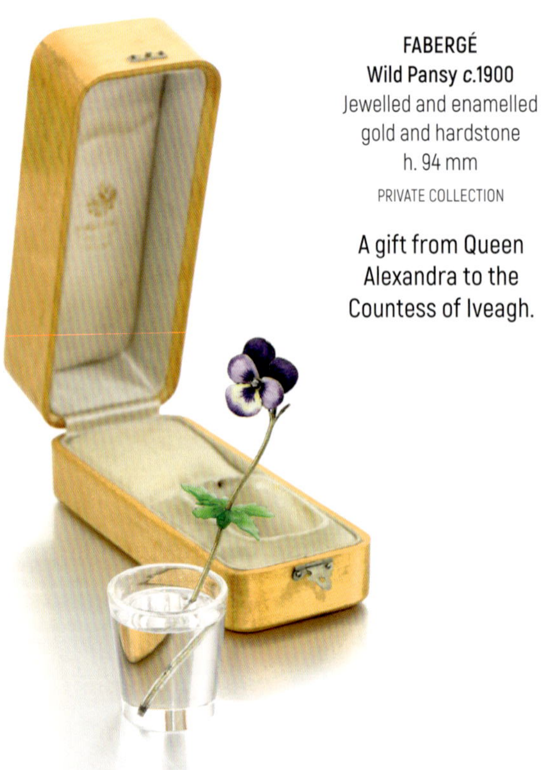

FABERGÉ
Wild Pansy c.1900
Jewelled and enamelled gold and hardstone
h. 94 mm
PRIVATE COLLECTION

A gift from Queen Alexandra to the Countess of Iveagh.

There were Norfolk precedents for dramatic dispersals in the wake of crippling debt, chief among them being losses to Prime Minister Sir Robert Walpole's legacy at Houghton. Sandringham estate borders the Houghton estate, which successive Marquesses of Cholmondeley – direct descendants of Sir Robert – had left dust-sheeted or tenanted. But they retained the title of hereditary joint Lord Great Chamberlain, taking charge of the Palace of Westminster and featuring in formal state occasions for

Elveden Hall house party January 1910. Edward VII is at the centre of this group and Mrs Keppel is seated far left

COURTESY OF THE EARL OF IVEAGH

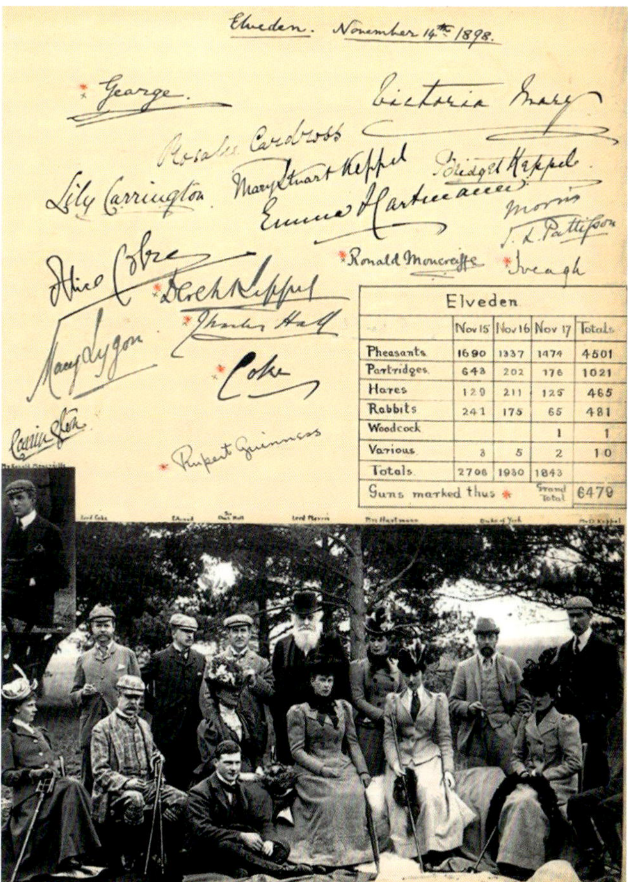

Elveden. November 14th 1898.

George. Victoria Mary
Rosalie Cardross
Lily Carrington Mary Stuart Keppel Bridget Keppel
Emma Hartmann
Morris
J. L. Pattisson
Ronald Moncreiffe Iveagh
Alice Coke
Derek Keppel
Thomas Hall
Mary Lygon
Coke
Rupert Guinness

Elveden	Nov 15	Nov 16	Nov 17	Totals
Pheasants	1690	1337	1474	4501
Partridges	643	202	176	1021
Hares	129	211	125	465
Rabbits	241	175	65	481
Woodcock			1	1
Various	3	5	2	10
Totals	2706	1930	1843	
Guns marked thus *			Grand Total	6479

Elveden Hall shooting party including the Duke and Duchess of York (the future George V and Queen Mary)

COURTESY OF THE EARL OF IVEAGH

every alternate reign. The 4th Marquess exercised the office during the era of Edward VII, also hosting the King and Queen at Houghton. Sir Robert had commissioned the Palladian gem from the 1720s, and employed an army of artists and craftsmen, led by furniture designer William Kent, to decorate it. He then brought in more than 400 Old Master paintings: 20 Van Dycks, 19 Rubenses, eight Titians, five Murillos, three Poussins, two Velázquez and a Raphael. There were further works by Claude Lorrain, Rembrandt, Frans Hals, Jan van Huysum, Salvator Rosa and Guido Reni, plus a roomful by Carlo Maratta. Sir Robert was created Earl of Orford in 1742, after ending a record 21-year term as Prime Minister. But his death three years later left enormous debts. In 1779 his grandson, George Walpole, 3rd Earl of Orford, sold 204 paintings – not, alas, to a National Gallery in London (that would not be founded until 1824). They went, for £40,555 (£50 million today), to Catherine the Great of Russia, who added a huge portrait of herself as a token of thanks. She boasted that all those masterpieces would vanish into her palaces, where only she 'and the mice' would ever see them; but millions have enjoyed them since 1852 in what is now the State Hermitage Museum. Had they stayed put in Norfolk, many would have been lost when Houghton's picture gallery was devastated by fire. Houghton itself survived, to be magnificently revived in the 20th century, and today it is a showcase for major collections of historical and modern art.

But perhaps among all of Norfolk's stately homes, save for Sandringham, Bertie liked Quidenham Hall best. At this seat of the Earls of Albemarle, in 1898, he met the wife of the third son of the 7th Earl: Alice Keppel. She became his mistress soon afterwards, the bond lasting for the final 12 years of his life. The house is now a Carmelite nunnery and long home to art critic and anchorite Sister Wendy Beckett.

After Alexander Roslin
Catherine the Great before 1780
Oil on canvas
THE MARQUESS OF CHOLMONDELEY

FABERGÉ
Workmaster Henrik Wigström
Golden Pheasant *c.* 1903–1908
Tiger's eye quartz, rose diamonds, gold
h. 43 x w. 70 x d. 21 mm
ROYAL COLLECTION TRUST

FABERGÉ
Cock Pheasant *c.* 1907
Agate, rose diamonds, gold
h. 33 x w. 62 x d. 21 mm
ROYAL COLLECTION TRUST

Present in pre-Norman Conquest England, the common or ring-necked pheasant surged after the Game Act of 1831 set up a system of licences, keepers and close seasons. Massive numbers bred on East Anglian estates augmented the wild population. Golden or Chinese pheasants were also established as ornamental and game birds from Victorian times

CHAPTER FIVE

The Bird Market

Birds besotted Fabergé, his patrons and the age. In keeping with their taxonomic vision of existence, the Victorians developed the science of ornithology and it reflected their treatment of the natural world generally.

The Victorian era saw an explosion of interest in natural history, geology and theories of evolution – with fossil-hunters poking and prodding the fields and cliffs of Norfolk, and Sir Alfred Jodrell, the county's High Sheriff in 1887, forming a global collection of shells and other curios over six decades, first in his home at Bayfield Hall, near Holt, and then in Glandford Shell Museum. Wildflower-pickers and pressers stalked marshes, heaths and meadows alongside naturalists armed with butterfly nets and chloroform jars (the swallowtail butterfly of fenland and broadland being particularly prized).

Eloise Harriet Stannard
1829–1915
Dying Birds 1874
Oil on canvas
h. 231 x w. 382 mm
NORWICH CASTLE MUSEUM AND ART GALLERY

Best known for her Dutch-inspired studies of fruits and flowers, still-life painter Eloise Harriet Stannard was one of two notable women linked to the 19th-century Norwich School of Artists.

FABERGÉ
Woodcock 1908–1917
Silver, green marble
h. 86 x w. 170 x d. 95 mm
ROYAL COLLECTION TRUST

This woodcock paperweight was not part of the Sandringham commission. But it depicts a prized asset of the Norfolk shooting estate. Elusive woodland birds, woodcock benefited from pheasant coverts planted from the 1830s, while also being bagged on pheasant shoots. Britain's breeding population, now dipping towards 50,000 pairs, is augmented by as many as 1.5 million autumn migrants from Scandinavia and Russia.

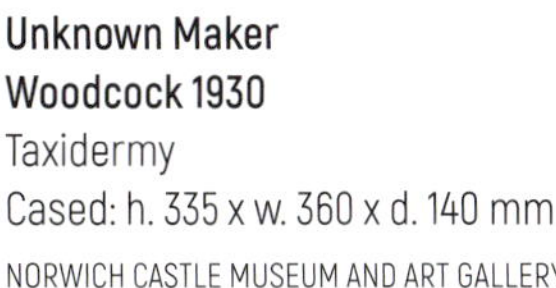

Unknown Maker
Woodcock 1930
Taxidermy
Cased: h. 335 x w. 360 x d. 140 mm
NORWICH CASTLE MUSEUM AND ART GALLERY

The pursuit of knowledge and killing so often went hand-in-hand – not least among members of the clergy. Eggs were blown and birds were blasted for their plumage rather than their flesh. Rarity was a trigger for slaughter. In 1856 alone the *Norfolk Chronicle* reported:

> *A male specimen of Savi's warbler, the rarest of British marsh warblers, was shot near Brundall. This is the only bird of the species obtained in the county since 1842, when a pair were killed at South Walsham, which, with one in the Norwich Museum, are all that are known to have occurred in Norfolk. The one in the Museum was obtained by the Rev. James Brown, at Limpenhoe, in the early part of the century.*

A white stork was shot in the plantation of Mr H.H. Saye, at North Pickenham. Its wings measured 6 ft. 3 in. from tip to tip, it was 4 ft. in length, and weighed 8 lbs. The bird was preserved by Mr T. Ellis, of Swaffham.

A sea eagle was shot at Winterton. It measured from its beak to its tail 3 ft., and from tip to top of its wings 8 ft.

And in June 1869 the *Norfolk Chronicle* further revealed:

> *A crane was shot at South Pickenham. It was a young male. In good condition, measured 64 inches in length, and weighed 10½lbs.; the expanse of its wings was 93 inches. On the 12th two were killed out of four seen at Burnham, and about the same time another was shot on the Thornham salt marshes. The occurrence of so many cranes in one year was remarkable, as not more than three or four specimens were known to have been procured in Norfolk during the preceding half century.*

To so many naturalists in Victorian East Anglia the word 'preservation' meant the art of taxidermy. The most noted among a large flock of animal-stuffers was Thomas Edward Gunn (1844–1923), a founder member of the Norfolk and Norwich Naturalists' Society. He long ran the biggest and most bemedalled taxidermy enterprise in Norwich, in St Giles Street. Ebonised pine boxes were lined with paper perhaps painted a sky blue and decorated with dried flowers and foliage around the central figures of stuffed fish, mammals and, especially, birds. Kingfishers, hoopoes and golden orioles were among prized species, as were raptors (particularly hen and marsh harriers) and terns. The last of these, the most ancient of birds related to prehistoric pterodactyls, faced a new threat by late-Victorian times: their wings and entire bodies were gathered for a new style in ladies' hats. As a result of this fashion, nesting little terns were lost to coastal Norfolk until they recolonised Blakeney Point and elsewhere later in the 20th century. Fen drainage, more than fashion, wiped out the bittern for nearly 60 years from 1850, but herons were massacred in vast numbers to provide feathers for millinery trimmings.

Taxidermist
Thomas Edward Gunn
1844–1923
PRIVATE COLLECTION

Thomas Edward Gunn
Stoat 1919
Taxidermy
Cased: h. 280 x w. 410 x d. 125 mm
NORWICH CASTLE MUSEUM AND ART GALLERY

FABERGÉ
Corncrake on a Wheatsheaf 1907
Chalcedony, rose diamonds
h. 30 x w. 70 x d. 40 mm
ROYAL COLLECTION TRUST

In 1907 the rasping call of the male corncrake filled summer evenings across the East Anglian countryside. Mechanised farming then saw the bird wiped out across mainland Britain until 2000, when Norfolk's Pensthorpe Conservation Trust hatched a reintroduction programme in the Cambridgeshire fens.

FABERGÉ
Stoat *c.* 1907
Opal, cabochon rubies
h. 10 x w. 27 x d. 10 mm
ROYAL COLLECTION TRUST

Although targeted by gamekeepers, stoats and weasels were plentiful in Edwardian East Anglia – as they are today.

CHAPTER SIX

The Daughter of Albion

Alexandra Feodorovna – daughter of Princess Alice, Grand Duchess of Hesse and the Rhine, and a favourite granddaughter of Queen Victoria – was in many ways an Englishwoman abroad. French had been the language of the St Petersburg court since the city's foundation along Western lines by Peter the Great in 1703, and Russian aristocrats came to regard the native tongue as the preserve of peasants and servants. But the new Empress could speak French little better than the Russian she could barely speak at all, and much preferred to converse in English (she and Nicholas would write to each other in English for the rest of their lives). That set a fashion. A city long hosting a community of British traders was soon rife with English tutors – as charted in the 1977 book *When Miss Emmie was in Russia: English governesses before, during and after the October Revolution* by Norfolk's Harvey Pitcher. The title honours Emma Dashwood, the author's Cromer neighbour, who shared terrific and terrible memories as one of a band of intrepid young East Anglian women who taught in the mansions of imperial Russia. Governesses in Britain endured poor pay and low status. Better prospects abroad fed the spirit of adventure.

The English governess in Russia was frequently placed on a similar social footing to her employers. She might end as companion rather than servant. Most expat governesses were shielded from Great War carnage, but all came to know the terror and famine that followed the Bolshevik Revolution of October 1917. Confident that Britain would eventually come to their rescue, they remained loyal, resourceful, resilient and brave – some taking sole charge of the children in their care when parents were killed, imprisoned or in hiding. There were ghastly journeys, risking robbery and murder, and amazing escapes in the chaos of civil war. One East Anglian, Helen Clarke, got safely home, only to set out again to save her Russian family. Miss Emmie sailed on a British ship from Crimea as the Red Army roared in.

Léopold Bernstamm for Sèvres Porcelain Manufactory Nicholas II 1897
Porcelain
h. 480 mm
ANDRE RUZHNIKOV

Nicholai Kirsanov for the Imperial Porcelain Factory Empress Alexandra Feodorovna *c.* 1896
Porcelain
h. 700 mm
ANDRE RUZHNIKOV

FABERGÉ
Tea set with samovar 1899–1908
Silver and ivory
Samovar and stand: h. 553 x 368 mm
PRIVATE COLLECTION, NORFOLK

Emma Dashwood had gone to Russia with her friend Gertrude Kirby. They stayed initially with Edith Kovalsky (née Sinclair), a fellow native of Norwich who had married a naval officer in St Petersburg and had come to provide a first port of call and unofficial employment agency for family and friends from Norfolk. Edith taught Emmie (and Gertie) how to behave in polite Russian society – with great social store being set on an ability to officiate at the samovar. As Harvey Pitcher writes of this helpful prop for any English governess:

> *Instead of sitting uncomfortably at the table unable to take any part in the conversation, she would feel more at ease doing something useful and exchanging a few Russian words, however limited in scope, with the visitors. The nickel samovar would be brought in and placed in front of her. The charcoal used for keeping the water on the boil all the time could be seen at the bottom glowing a bright red, while the boiling water inside hissed and whined in a cheerful singsong. On top, keeping warm, stood a small teapot containing very, very strong China tea. There was quite an art in judging when to fill up the teapot and how long to let it stand, while at the same time trying to make polite if stumbling conversation with a visitor.*

FABERGÉ
Workmaster Henrik Wigström
Panagia *c.* 1910
Gold, diamonds, sapphires, pearls, enamel
h. 152 mm x w. 86 mm; medallion:
44 x 38 mm; chain 457 mm
A LA VIEILLE RUSSIE, NEW YORK

Wearing a Panagia, or icon pendant, distinguishes an Orthodox bishop from other clergy. In a setting of gold, diamond, sapphires and pearls, this fine cloisonné enamel medallion of Christ Pantocrator is based on an 11th-century Byzantine image now in New York's Metropolitan Museum of Art

FABERGÉ
Workmaster Mikhail Perkhin
Triptych Icon given 1895
Silver, enamel, emeralds, sapphires, pearls, birch
h. 254 x w. 324 mm
A LA VIEILLE RUSSIE, NEW YORK

This Byzantine-style triptych icon was given by the St Petersburg nobility to Tsar Nicholas II and Empress Alexandra in November 1895, on the birth of their first child, Grand Duchess Olga. The central panel portrays their patron saints. The bejewelled and birch-panelled exterior represents a church steeple.

CHAPTER SEVEN

Bad Weather

Storms in January 1905 kept fishing boats in east-coast harbours, including the hundreds of vessels lined bow-to-bow along Fisher Fleet in the ancient seaport of King's Lynn. Crews unable to get out on The Wash repaired to Pilot Street pubs at the heart of a self-contained North End fishing community, ranged within a few streets' radius of St Nicholas Chapel, also known as the fishermen's church. Here, drinking and singing, they waited for the weather to change and altered the course of English classical music. For among them, taking notes, was the composer Ralph Vaughan Williams (1872–1958). He had collected his first folk song, 'Bushes and Briars', from an elderly farm labourer in Essex the previous winter, and such traditional ditties (over time he would harvest more than 800) had already influenced his atmospheric homage to East Anglia, the 'symphonic impression' called *In the Fen Country*. Now, in the Tilden Smith bar, mariners such as Duggie Carter and Joe Anderson belted out the sea shanties they had learned by heart from their fathers and grandfathers. Tunes for 'The Captain's Apprentice', 'A Bold Young Sailor' and 'On Board a Ninety-Eight' were then woven like a net through the first of three orchestral *Norfolk Rhapsodies* by Vaughan Williams.

What was meant to be the opening movement of a Norfolk symphony was premiered in London in August 1906 and revised in 1914 – the year of 'The Lark Ascending' – before the outbreak of war that summer and the composer's enlistment on New Year's Eve. By that point the Second and Third Rhapsodies had been performed and withdrawn. While the middle movement survives as a fragment, the final part is lost. So *Norfolk Rhapsody No. 1* in E minor now has an air of completion its creator had not intended. Inspired in a public house within 10 miles (16 kilometres) of, and a world away from, Sandringham, the piece evokes similar feelings about an English idyll and how it was swept away as does the Fabergé commission to depict the animals on a model estate. But a sense of melancholy pervaded the Norfolk rhapsody from the outset. The old tars who sang it as they sat out the storm, amid lives of dire hardship and recurrent danger reflected in the threnody of their music, would have worn the North End's distinctive gansey sweaters. Traditionally, East Anglian sailors never learned to swim, so that they might drown more quickly in the event of disaster at sea. The pattern on their knitted jumpers was designed to identify their place of origin when bodies were washed up on shores far from home.

In 1919 Vaughan Williams settled in Sheringham to write *A Pastoral Symphony*, which, despite its name, reflected on the First World War killing fields of France he had experienced as an ambulance driver and a lieutenant in the Royal Artillery. Ultimately he was to be deafened by the noise of the guns.

Ralph Vaughan Williams around 1905

CHAPTER EIGHT

White Nights

Sofka Dolgorouky (1907–1994) was the granddaughter of Minny's best friend, and claimed descent through her warring parents from both Catherine the Great and Rurik, Prince of Kiev. In exile, the blue-blooded rebel embraced bohemianism and finally Bolshevism, before publishing her autobiography in the suitably tumultuous year of 1968; but her astonishing life story made for an even more riveting read in the 2007 best-seller *Red Princess: A Revolutionary Life*, written by her own granddaughter, Sofka Zinovieff.

The Princess was conceived immediately after the January 1907 wedding, held in the private church of the Winter Palace, which united two of Russia's noblest families and saw Romanovs massed in attendance. She played with the Tsarevich, witnessed the revolution and then escaped with her Dolgorouky grandmother to Crimea, where they awaited their fate alongside Minny. At Easter 1918 the Dowager Empress gave the spirited child a tiny Fabergé egg, which remains in the Zinovieff family to this day.

But back in 1907, the birth of Sofka Dolgorouky had coincided with a moment of great hope for Russia. As Sofka Zinovieff writes in *Red Princess*:

This was an extraordinary time. Russia was richer than ever before, trade was booming and the revolutionary terrorists had gone relatively quiet. People were already starting to forget the humiliating defeat in the war with Japan, and the carnage of 1905 with Bloody Sunday, when troops and police fired on a peaceful demonstration of workers. Liberals were still hopeful that the country could reform itself, while revolutionaries got depressed; Lenin (in exile) kept complaining that he'd never live to see the revolution.

St Petersburg was witnessing the height of the cultural blossoming known as the Silver Age. Russia's painters, poets, writers, musicians and dancers were now leading European trends and it was hard to keep up with the latest movement; Symbolists, Modernists, Acmeists and Futurists competed for attention with dilettanti, rebels, revolutionaries, pamphleteers, pornographers, Bohemians ... Court circles may not have taken much notice, but St Petersburg was in a ferment; a last mad flowering before it was all swept away by war and revolution.

FABERGÉ

Varvara Panina *c.* 1902

Aventurine quartz, jasper, quartz, purpurine, calcite, and other Russian hardstones, diamonds, gold, silver

h. 178 mm

A LA VIEILLE RUSSIE, NEW YORK

This portrait of singer Varvara Panina (1872–1911) is the largest and best-known of around 60 Fabergé hardstone figures. With a voice like Edith Piaf, her passionate rendition of Romany folk songs and Russian romances thrilled both the Romanov court and the masses.

Anna Pavlova dancing
The Dying Swan

St Petersburg-born Anna Pavlova (1881–1931) caused a sensation when dancing *The Dying Swan* to Mikhail Fokine's revolutionary choreography. She was first filmed in her signature role in 1907, the year of Fabergé's Sandringham commission.

Ballet was one of the art forms bringing Britain and Russia together. Pavlova danced in London in 1910, and the following year Diaghilev brought the Imperial Russian Ballet – with Karsavina and Nijinsky – to Covent Garden, for a triumph reprised in 1912. Décor and costumes by distinguished artists – Leon Bakst, Alexandre Benois and Natalia Goncharova – were as exciting as the dancing and set new trends in fashion and interior design, greatly influencing Roger Fry's Omega Workshops.

Ballet stars were feted with Fabergé gifts. Anna Pavlova received this stickpin after dancing for the Russian Royal Family at the Winter Palace.

FABERGÉ
Stickpin 1898
Gold, enamel, diamonds
l. 83 mm
A LA VIEILLE RUSSIE, NEW YORK

FABERGÉ
Swan *c.* 1898
Pearl, diamonds, gold
l. 61 mm
A LA VIEILLE RUSSIE, NEW YORK

К.ФАБЕРЖЕ

Born at Blofield, near Norwich, John Emms served as studio assistant in London to Frederic, Lord Leighton, before winning fame and fortune as late-Victorian Britain's best-loved dog painter.

This Emms painting shows the Duchess of Newcastle's dogs, Nagrajdai, Oudar, Golub and Ooslad. Oudar was bought for £200 from Tsar Alexander III after being shown at Crufts in 1892.

John Emms
1843–1912
Four of the Duchess of Newcastle's Borzoi 1892
Oil on canvas
h. 1015 x w. 1525 mm
REPRODUCED WITH KIND PERMISSION OF THE KENNEL CLUB

FABERGÉ
Borzoi *c.* 1908
Agate, rubies
h. 54 x w. 68 x d. 15 mm
ROYAL COLLECTION TRUST

FABERGÉ
Vassilka 1908
Silver, aventurine quartz
h. 134 x w. 211 x d. 90 mm
ROYAL COLLECTION TRUST

Vassilka and Alex, a pair of borzoi or Russian wolfhounds, were presents from the Russian royal family to their British relatives. They probably began the breeding of borzoi from the Sandringham Kennels, and the resulting exhibition of wolfhounds, for which Alexandra became noted. Vassilka won more than 75 prizes – including Best Dog at the Norwich Kennel Club Show.

CHAPTER NINE

A Country Cottage

Victoria and Albert were early patrons of photography. They both learned how to produce calotypes and had a darkroom built at Windsor Castle. They approved publication of a first photographic image of themselves and their nine children in 1857, to promote the royal example of family values on which they believed the future of the monarchy rested – appealing to the expanding middle classes against threats of republicanism and revolution. The Duke of York, though the despair of his parents, would come to extol public duty over private virtue – exhibiting tact, charm and an invaluable memory for names and faces, which eventually made him a highly popular monarch. His jovial figure, reproduced in countless photographs in the latter decades of the 19th century, appeared to stand for a new era of goodwill, generosity and enjoyment awaiting in a new century.

The costly art of photography was long the preserve of the upper classes, a fact exploited by Fabergé in a lavish array of photograph frames. Like her relatives in Russia, Alix became an accomplished photographer – *Queen Alexandra's Christmas Gift Book: Photographs from my Camera*, a fund-raiser for charity, with images of family gatherings at home and abroad, being a 1908 festive best-seller. She also compiled many private albums, with some further displaying her skills as a collagist and watercolourist. Several volumes included Norfolk scenes, and one recorded horses and mares at the Sandringham Stud from 1887 to 1917.

At Sandringham, armed successively with Numbers 1, 2 and 4 Kodak box cameras, Alexandra was assisted in her hobby by Frederick William Ralph (1836–1919). He had been a teenage farmhand when entering the royal household, in 1863, as 'usher of the servants' hall'. In a 1902 interview with the *Westminster Gazette* he said he had taught the then Queen to take, develop and print her own images. He had also come to combine servant duties at Sandringham with a commercial photography business, producing popular postcards of the royal estate and surrounding area. Special access to the royal family for his own portrait photos was a long-established fact when Frederick received a Royal Warrant as Photographer to King Edward VII in 1904, later continued by George V. The slogan 'By appointment to HM the King' then appeared in F.W. Ralph's studio windows in Dersingham and Hunstanton. What became a flourishing family enterprise also involved his daughter, Beatrice, and sons Frederick and Walter.

Edward and Caesar 1910
Postcard
PRIVATE COLLECTION, SUFFOLK

Prince George (1865–1936) would also honeymoon at Sandringham, in 1893, even though his bride, Princess Mary (May) of Teck, had formerly been engaged to his beloved elder brother, Albert Victor, Duke of Clarence and Avondale, who had died there 18 months earlier. They began married life in the cramped confines of York Cottage, and it remained their Norfolk home until Sandringham House was vacated, in 1925, by Alexandra's death, 15 years into George's reign. Today it is the Sandringham Estate Office. As Duke of York, George had declined his father's offer to rent Houghton Hall for him. He was happy in his country cottage – and his wife, despite a taste for palaces and the grandest connoisseur's possessions, made the best of it. There was no place like Sandringham for both Prince and King George, and he died there in 1936 – having, almost uniquely among leading members of the royal family, never learned to speak a foreign language. As this model of a Victorian Norfolk squire once said: 'Abroad is awful. I know. I've been.'

Frederick William Ralph
1836–1919
Royal family group 1889
Albumen cabinet card
h. 82 x w. 82 mm
NATIONAL PORTRAIT GALLERY

Here Alexandra (second from left) is seen at Sandringham with her son, the future George V, and daughters Louise, Victoria and Maud, plus attendant dogs. All the humans, and perhaps the canines too, loved the Norfolk estate like nowhere else.

Often overshadowed by the loving and clinging, charismatic and eclipsing matriarch they all called 'Motherdear', the three princesses were most free and high-spirited in the privacy of Sandringham. After wary public appearances in adulthood, they came to be dubbed 'Their Royal Shynesses' and, more cruelly, 'The Hags'.

Victoria (1868–1935) never married and became her widowed mother's put-upon companion. Louise, later Princess Royal and Duchess of Fife (1867–1931), often returned to Sandringham. Maud (1869–1938) never really left. In 1896 she married her Danish cousin, Charles, and ten years later they became Queen Maud and King Haakon VII of Norway. They had honeymooned at Appleton House on the Sandringham estate, which her parents had given them as a wedding present. To Maud, it was to be her home forever. She returned for at least three prolonged visits each year and died there, two years before her widower and their Sandringham-born son, Crown Prince Olaf, fled Norway for Britain following a German invasion. Appleton House was demolished in the 1980s.

CHAPTER TEN

Rapture

In the 1949 book about his life in the Fabergé enterprise, former London branch manager Henry Bainbridge recalled the demanding task of serving royalty successfully, and one telling episode in particular. He wrote:

> *Working to please King Edward should have taught me one lesson, that whatever you suggested to him he would go one better. But in one's eagerness to take full advantage of the craftsmanship of Fabergé one never learned the lesson, so I was never out of one difficulty before I was plunged into another. And the biggest of all came with the proposal to model a few of the favourite animals at Sandringham and then cut them into different stones in the colours of the originals.*

A man never lacking in self-esteem, Bainbridge credited himself with the proposal. According to him, he had already spoken to zoologist Sir Ray Lankester, then director of the Natural History Museum, about a vastly ambitious scheme to encourage the breeders of English pedigrees to have portraits of their animals in stone, bronze or silver; but nothing had come of it – so the branch manager had kept the idea in his head for a more limited use. What he didn't mention was that Queen Alexandra had already applauded Alfred Lyndhurst Pocock's models of some of her own prized pets and, in so doing, signalled that a wider Sandringham commission would be welcome. Bainbridge also knew from experience that the Queen preferred the more modest Fabergé's pieces, being relatively affordable and therefore both giveable and receivable as gifts without any fear of embarrassment or offence, and that she loved the animals and flowers best of all.

Bainbridge said he had raised the question of royal animal studies in his shop with Mrs Keppel, and she had suggested a small group of Sandringham favourites to add to the Queen's Fabergé collection. Together they imagined a project covering a few dogs and horses, if the King approved. He duly did – as Bainbridge remembered:

FABERGÉ
Cairn Terrier *c.* 1907
Agate, rose diamonds
h. 45 x w. 60 x d. 18 mm
ROYAL COLLECTION TRUST

FABERGÉ
Pug *c.* 1907
Agate, rose diamonds
h. 50 x w. 47 x d. 20 mm
ROYAL COLLECTION TRUST

FABERGÉ
Border Terrier *c.* 1907–1908
Agate, rose diamonds
h. 31 x w. 50 x d. 19 mm
ROYAL COLLECTION TRUST

FABERGÉ
Pig *c.* 1907
Agate, diamonds
h. 30 x w. 74 x d. 47 mm
ROYAL COLLECTION TRUST

There are 19 pigs or piglets in the Royal Collection, several of them linked to the Sandringham commission. Edward VII was also a pig fan, leading any willing visitor to admire the 'improved Norfolks' at the Home Farm.

FABERGÉ
Large White Sow *c.* 1907
Aventurine quartz, rose diamonds
h. 72 x w. 147 x d. 75 mm
ROYAL COLLECTION TRUST

Next day I received a telegram from Sandringham, 'The King agrees; Mr Beck [the land agent] will make all the arrangements', and so I took the next train to Wolferton. As usual, things were going far too well to begin with and my guardian angel was at the winning-post long before I was half-way there; for I learned from the King's agent that not only were Persimmon, the King's Derby winner, Caesar, his favourite rough-haired terrier, and one or two of the Queen's dogs, to be done, but as Mr Beck put it, 'the whole farmyard', heifers and bullocks, cocks and hens, turkeys, shire horses and even pigs.

At a stroke, the King had gone twenty better and this time I was really in the welter of the impossible. As I journeyed back to London I wondered how I would tell Fabergé, for as yet he knew nothing about it. How would he find stones enough? What about the cost of the venture? How about the modellers; could they be spared to work in this country for months? All the precious nonsense of portrait models in rare stones sounded well enough, but suppose the whole thing turned out a fiasco? And with the King of England, too!

On their orders Edward's and Alexandra's personal papers were destroyed after their deaths, and many of Fabergé's records are also lost, so documentation for this extraordinary episode in the history of East Anglian art is sadly meagre. What is clear is that the largest order ever placed through Fabergé's London branch ultimately resulted in the biggest assemblage in existence of the firm's hardstone animal sculptures. Most are now in the British Royal Collection – from which a record tally of more than 50 animals has been lent to the Sainsbury Centre exhibition accompanying this book. At least twice that number of models have been linked to the project – and the *Black shire horse* lent to the Norwich show from America is among them. Royal Collection curator Caroline de Guitaut, author of *Fabergé's Animals: A Royal Farm in Miniature*, has compiled a register based on 'known portraits, date of production, breeds native to East Anglia and examples of animals known to have inhabited the estate at Sandringham, together with the records of purchases made through the London branch'. Animals featured here are on that list. Some may well have followed on from the original commission, as Fabergé tilted production towards the taste of Britain's Queen, and towards animal types in Norfolk. A recent *Fabergé in London* book by Kieran McCarthy – director of Wartski, which has dealt in Fabergé since the 1920s, first in Llandudno and then in London – draws on the previously unseen Bainbridge papers, to suggest that the number of finished figures resulting directly from the Sandringham commission was fewer than two dozen.

Answering the royal summons, Fabergé sent to Norfolk his best animal sculptors, and further drafted in one of his sons, to ensure the success of a plum venture taking several months to reach fruition. According to Bainbridge's published account, Swiss-born, London-based Frank Lutiger and unnamed others joined Boris Frödman-Cluzel, who was of Swedish and French parentage, but grew up and resided in St Petersburg. Once in Norfolk, and with their initial works delighting

FABERGÉ
Sheep *c.* 1907
Agate, rose diamonds
h. 40 x w. 71 x d. 36 mm
ROYAL COLLECTION TRUST

On an 1869 Nile cruise Alexandra rescued a runaway black long-tailed sheep from the lunch menu and as a Sandringham pet it became a favourite with the royal children. Several sheep breeds were kept on the Norfolk estate. This sole ovine model from the Fabergé commission shows a Southdown ram.

FABERGÉ
Black shire horse 1907
Obsidian, cabochon rubies, gold
l. 149 mm
A LA VIEILLE RUSSIE, NEW YORK

This shire horse with golden bridle belonged to Sandringham-born Prince Henry, Duke of Gloucester (1900–1974), third son of King George and Queen Mary, until its sale at Christie's in 1954. It has been reunited with other animals linked to the Sandringham commission for the Sainsbury Centre exhibition.

both Edward and Alexandra, the sculptors are believed to have been further detained by a royal command to portray not only the farmyard, as outlined by Frank Beck, but pet and wild animals also dear to the Queen's heart.

Nicholas Fabergé, Carl Fabergé's youngest son, had another reason for dallying. Writing in Frank and Mary Beck's Visitors Book, on New Year's Eve, 21-year-old Nicholas recalled 'the happiest and most enjoyable X-mas holidays I've had since I left my country 5 years ago'. His adventures abroad had lately culminated in a position as joint-manager of the London branch (a fact Mr Bainbridge neglected to mention in his own account), so his role in the Sandringham commission may have been substantial. But his main reason for wanting to linger in Norfolk was that he had fallen in love with the Becks' 15-year-old daughter Margaretta, known as Meg. Their romance, if it had even begun, was to prove short-lived, however. He wrote her a letter declaring his love, which was posted to Meg's school – where it was opened by her headmistress, who also happened to be her unmarried aunt. Further contact was forbidden, and they never met again. Meg was married at Sandringham in 1922 – an event key to a later part of this story.

But posterity should cheer H.C. Bainbridge for leaving us with the intoxicating drama of the Sandringham saga (if not always the sober truth). As his memoir continued:

> *I was only at the beginning of my Fabergé in Wonderland. Nobody was to be in it to the same extent as myself. The King was to have his portion, Fabergé his but as luck would have it the beginning, the middle and the end were to be mine alone. The last-minute telegrams from Sandringham on the eve of the Queen's birthday, the midnight drives through the woods of Wolferton, with prancing horses, a royal coachman and footman all complete, the reception at Sandringham House by some important personage, as though I were some last minute saviour of a desperate situation. 'While you are having something to eat, I will unpack your bag.' So said King George of Greece, Queen Alexandra's brother, the last time I saw him on one of these excursions.*

Whatever his shortcomings as a reliable witness, the Bainbridge description of the final presentation of wax maquettes in the Model Dairy, on 8 December 1907, conjures up a wonderfully theatrical scene:

> *If on that day, shortly after lunch, you had found yourself, as I did, hiding behind a hedge in the grounds of Sandringham, you would have seen the King leaving Sandringham House surrounded by his guests. He was dressed in a tight-fitting overcoat and what looked like a small cricket cap. It was very evident something was astir, for the whole party was moving at a pace as though there were no time to lose, and Caesar, the King's terrier, added zest by rushing in and out, barking all the time . . .*
>
> *For months past Fabergé's artists had been hard at work modelling the animals according to the King's list: Boris Frödman-Cluzel, Frank Lutiger and others, unfortunately not now remembered. During the time they had been at work they had become what can be best described as the Sandringham Star Turn. On shooting days, by the King's command, all work ceased and he took the artists round with him and, at the usual royal gathering for luncheon, presented them to the Queen, the Prince and Princess of Wales and his guests. In many other ways he showed that spirit which was essentially his, of extracting from a situation all there was to get.*
>
> *And never did he show it better than on that Sunday afternoon in December 1907, when at his command all the finished wax models were set out in the Queen's Dairy for his examination and criticism. His cosmopolitanism joined hands with his love of his home, and out of the union he contrived to stage a pageant. The incongruous combination of interests and people; the butter beautifully set out in one room of the dairy, awaiting the King's approval; in the other, artists of several nationalities keeping guard over their work and waiting, no doubt rather nervously, for the King's criticisms; the many guests split up into groups, strolling about outside the dairy and seemingly quite in the dark about what the King was up to; the setting of the scene in the Sandringham stable-yard, with Persimmon close by in his loose-box, perhaps wondering what was afoot; and the final gesture of the King, when standing on the steps of the dairy, he sent a message of congratulation to Carl Fabergé: 'Will you please tell Mr Fabergé how pleased I am with all he has done for me. I have pointed out to the artists one or two places where some little alteration can be made, but otherwise I think the work splendid.*

The reader is left to presume that Mr Bainbridge had at some point emerged from his hiding place behind the hedge to receive the positive royal verdict . . .

FABERGÉ
Workmaster Mikhail Perkhin
Parrot on a Perch 1896–1903
Agate, rose diamonds, gold, silver-gilt, guilloché enamel
h. 145 x w. 72 x d. 62 mm
ROYAL COLLECTION TRUST

Alexandra kept a variety of caged birds, including canaries and bullfinches, in her rooms at Sandringham, Marlborough House and Buckingham Palace. Edward had a pet parrot, which was moved from London to Norfolk.

FABERGÉ
Kitten *c.* 1907
Agate, rose Diamonds
h. 27 x w. 50 x d. 23 mm
ROYAL COLLECTION TRUST

Although famously devoted to dogs, Alexandra also doted on cats. On her 1901 tour of Sandringham, for *The Lady's Realm*, Sarah Tooley noted: 'In this stable a pet cat, "Selwood", has her little wooden house, and came forward to show her two lovely kittens. "Selwood" has also a corner at Marlborough House.'

FABERGÉ
Cat *c.* 1910
Jasper, olivines, gold
h. 56 x w. 50 x d. 19 mm
ROYAL COLLECTION TRUST

The Fabergé party had the run of the estate – stud and stables, Home Farm, gardens, park and swathes of estate beyond, where much wildlife lurked, despite the best efforts of gamekeepers. There would have been pets such as caged birds in the house, and racing pigeons in the royal loft. There were lots of cats – and dogs everywhere. Alix liked dogs of any breed and description, and she knew all the names and natures of the motley semi-residents of the 26 kennels close to the main house. She regularly fed her pets with cubes of bread, as shown in the Frederick Morgan and Thomas Blinks painting of 1902, *Queen Alexandra with Her Grandchildren and Dogs*. The kennels housed bulldogs and borzois, Great Danes and dachshunds, Pekingese, Chinese chows and Japanese chins (then known as Japanese spaniels), collies, pugs, poodles, Pomeranians, terriers and basset hounds. Plus the gundogs: Clumber spaniels and Labrador retrievers; and, resting after distant exertions, a Samoyed from an Arctic expedition and a Siberian sledge dog.

It's tempting to picture the Model Dairy – in the *cottage orné* style of rustic architecture popular in Britain since the late 18th century – as the scene not only for the final exhibition, but for much of the modelling too.

Frederick Morgan and Thomas Blinks
Queen Alexandra and her Grandchildren and Dogs 1902
Oil on canvas
h. 1665 x 2045 mm
ROYAL COLLECTION TRUST

This Sandringham scene from the year of Edward VII's Coronation shows Queen Alexandra with grandchildren Prince Albert (the future George VI), Prince Edward (Edward VIII) and Princess Mary, with Kennel Keeper Mr Brunsden and Collies Flo, Lochiel and Sandringham Nicety, Borzoi Alex, Deerhound Callac, Bassets Sandringham Gaiety and Sandringham Flora and Schipperke Chira.

FABERGÉ
Workmaster Henrik Wigström
Frame with a view of Sandringham Dairy *c.* 1911
Gold, enamel, sepia enamel, ivory
h. 46 x w. 71 x d. 21 mm
ROYAL COLLECTION TRUST

Model Dairy interior *c.* 1907
Postcard
PRIVATE COLLECTION, SUFFOLK

Model Dairy *c.* 1907
Postcard
PRIIVATE COLLECTION, SUFFOLK

It features in one of three Fabergé frames with enamelled Sandringham views, now in the Royal Collection (others show the house and church). The main room, where Alix entertained guests to tea, would have been ideal for the project. Freely ranging across the Aesthetic, Symbolist and Arts and Crafts movements, eclectic plaques and figurines set against tiled walls reflected a love of nature and model agriculture, and a search for rustic simplicity amid all the stuff and stuffiness of late-Victorian royal life. There was perhaps a hint of the fragile idyll that was Marie Antoinette's Petit Trianon – lost, like the royal milkmaid herself, to the French Revolution. But the air was more of Merrie England, and the display of bright ceramics from the Minton factory was led by a pair of Herbert Wilson Foster chargers (large flat dishes), casting the then Prince of Wales as Henry VIII, and Alix (since none of the six wives was quite suitable) as herself, but in Tudor costume and attended by a white cat.

The Model Dairy stood in a 'Dutch-style' garden, with climbing roses, formal flowerbeds, topiary yews shaped as chickens and peacocks, and a tree planted by future Tsar Nicholas II on a youthful visit to Norfolk in 1874. A tour granted to readers of *Country Life*, in July 1902, revealed two workrooms beyond the salon where Alix liked to picnic. One held churns and dishes for milk preparation and cream separation – with shelves on tiled walls for 'pretty earthenware ornaments' in the form of cows and rabbits – and the second was for butter-making. The dairymaid had inherited her position from her mother. The anonymous writer continued:

Everything, it is true, is of the best, and yet everything is humble and simple. The cows are of the best breed, but not showyard beauties or even winners at milking trials. No parade is made of their milking capacity, though a quiet register is kept of their performances, and the more one enquires the more evident does it become that thoroughness characterises every department. Similarly the maid has no diplomas to boast of, but what is of more consequence is that she is absolute mistress of her work.

While members of the public were allowed to visit part of the Sandringham estate on Tuesdays and Fridays when the royal family was not in residence, journalists gained greater access. Charles Dickens, son and namesake of the novelist, wrote up 'A Run to Sandringham' in 1887, in the *All the Year Round* journal that he had inherited from his father. He admired dogs 'in all sorts and sizes' and a pair of shaggy bears in a bear-pit, and heard there were monkeys hereabouts, but didn't get to see them. He also noted introductions of black grouse, red deer and white fallow deer to the sporting estate.

In 1901 writer Sarah Tooley and photographer Frederick William Ralph gave readers of *The Lady's Realm* the tour that Fabergé sculptors would receive six years later. The morning allotted to meet the new Queen's

FABERGÉ
Workmaster Henrik Wigström
Duckling *c.* 1908
Chalcedony, cabochon rubies, gold
h. 34 x w. 33 x d. 22 mm
ROYAL COLLECTION TRUST

FABERGÉ
Workmaster Henrik Wigström
Hen *c.* 1908
Agate, rose diamonds, gold
h. 59 x w. 51 x d. 29 mm
ROYAL COLLECTION TRUST

FABERGÉ
Workmaster Henrik Wigström
Bantam Cockerel *c.* 1908
Obsidian, purpurine, jasper, rose diamonds, gold
h. 99 x w. 78 x d. 47 mm
ROYAL COLLECTION TRUST

FABERGÉ
Workmaster Henrik Wigström
Chick *c.* 1907
Chalcedony, cabochon rubies, gold
h. 31 x w. 28 x d. 27 m
ROYAL COLLECTION TRUST

pets had proved insufficient, so another had been added. Guided by Mr Jackson, 'a sturdy-looking, genial Norfolk man, who has been head-keeper at Sandringham for thirty years', the tour began with the pheasantry, 'the King's special hobby'. Next came the Queen's prized and prize-winning bantams. For all its period sentimentality and deference, the description of the reigning black Rosecomb Bantam cockerel might still be matched to the subsequent Fabergé model:

> *I was duly introduced to her favourite, a saucy little fellow with his black feathers shining like satin in the sunshine, and his pretty head, which he held aloft as a Queen's bantam should, surmounted by a brilliant rose-coloured comb, while his ears were white. He crowed with a truly royal air, and his wives, almost as handsome as himself, looked much charmed.*

The writer was still more charmed by a bantam carnival involving silver and golden Sebrights, black Pekins and the black-tailed Japanese variety, Scotch Greys and 'Duckwing game bantams, most elegant birds', as well as 'the black and red variety, saucy little birds that strutted about like soldiers'. The bantams paraded on ground formerly occupied by a bear-pit.

After touring the pheasant incubator, where 10,000 birds were hatched annually and where the Queen liked to 'fondle the tiny chicks and press their downy feathers against her cheek', the Tooley visit proceeded to the dove-house near the head-keeper's cottage, cared for by Mrs Jackson:

> *Many years ago, when Queen Alexandra visited Ireland, she received on landing the present of a white dove as an emblem of peace and goodwill. On her return to London she brought it a mate, and provided a home for it at Sandringham, where the pair raised a numerous progeny. The present inhabitants of the Queen's dove-house are direct descendants of the original pair; they are white, with eyes like pink coral. I made the acquaintance of 'Willie', a lovely dove specially trained for 'my lady's chamber', who for many years had its cage in the Queen's boudoir, and would perch on her finger and nestle on her shoulder and feed from her hand. I do not know how it quite came about but 'Willie' was wrongly christened; she ought to have received the feminine form of Wilhelmina. The Queen decided not to re-name her pet, so 'Willie' the dove remained. It is now getting too old for an indoor pet, and is to pass the remainder of its days in the dove-house while a young and lovely descendant is being trained for the Queen's boudoir. Her Majesty does not forget her old favourite, and frequently comes to see 'Willie', who immediately flies to her shoulder.*

Next, 'on an ornamental piece of water, with island and trees', Sarah Tooley encountered captive oystercatchers dining on limpets and companioned by three turtle doves, which Alexandra had found to be fellow passengers on the homeward crossing from her 1900 annual visit to Denmark. During the voyage 'the Queen said she would have them brought to Sandringham, lest they might come to grief'.

Dove house from *The Lady's Realm* magazine 1901

FABERGÉ
Pigeon *c.* 1907
Banded agate, cabochon rubies, gold
h. 44 x w. 50 x d. 20 mm
ROYAL COLLECTION TRUST

FABERGÉ
Pouter Pigeon *c.* 1908
Agate, rose diamonds, gold
h. 30 x w. 42 x d. 21 mm
ROYAL COLLECTION TRUST

Sandringham's pigeon loft began in 1886 with gifted birds from Leopold II, King of the Belgians. Edward VII was a keen pigeon-racer. So was his son, the future George V – though his birds first flew under the name of West Newton schoolmaster Walter Jones, perhaps to avoid offending Queen Victoria.

Birds from the royal loft were used as carrier pigeons in both world wars, with one, Royal Blue, winning the Dickin Medal for gallantry for its role in reporting a lost aircraft in 1940. The Sandringham pigeon loft, now holding up to 250 birds, with many national and international race winners, was renewed in 2015.

FABERGÉ
Dove 1908
Chalcedony, rose diamonds, gold
h. 47 x w. 41 x d. 33 mm
ROYAL COLLECTION TRUST

Then to the kennels – centrepiece of the Sandringham menagerie for Fabergé's modellers:

> *Once a week at least the Queen, when at Sandringham, makes a systematic tour of the kennels. She first goes into Mrs Jackson's cottage to have a large white apron put on, and thus arrayed she begins her round, accompanied by Mr Brundson, who has been for fifteen years the keeper of her pets, carrying bread, which has been previously cut up by Mrs Jackson and arranged in dainty, but capacious baskets . . .*
>
> *Prince Edward, who sometimes comes with 'Granny', is rather alarmed when he sees the big dogs bounding out of their kennels. The Queen is absolutely fearless where animals are concerned and has wonderful control over them. The most unmanageable of them will do her bidding at a word . . . Should there be a dog on the sick-list, the Queen will pay him special visits in hospital, and have his progress reported to her day by day. She constantly exhibits, and is much pleased when her pets obtain a prize. The medals from time to time awarded to Sandringham dogs are kept in glass cases in Mr Brundson's pretty parlour, and make a brave show.*
>
> *So far as her personal pets are concerned, Her Majesty at the present time favours small fancy dogs. Her quaint little Japanese spaniels, 'Billy' and 'Punchy', travel with her wherever she goes, sleep on silken cushions in her dressing-room, and one or other of them is invariably carried under her arm when she walks. 'Facey', a white and brown spaniel, was her constant companion for many years, and has been immortalized in Mr Luke Fildes' picture of 'The Princess of Wales' with this pet under her arm. One sees a copy of this painting in many homes around Sandringham and hanging in hospitals and institutions visited by the Queen. It is a favourite gift-picture with Her Majesty.*

Luke Fildes
1843–1927
Queen Alexandra 1894–1920
Oil on canvas
h. 1590 x w. 1336 x d. 125 mm
NATIONAL PORTRAIT GALLERY

This Fildes portrait of Queen Alexandra with Punch, her beloved Japanese Chin, was commissioned by her son George V in 1920 as a copy of the picture painted in 1894 for his wedding.

FABERGÉ
Sandringham Lucy *c.* 1907
Chalcedony, rubies
h. 44 x w. 105 x d. 36 mm
ROYAL COLLECTION TRUST

Clumber spaniels were gundogs for Edward VII and his son George V. Sandringham Lucy, as portrayed in this ruby-eyed model bought from Fabergé's London shop by George in 1909, for the princely sum of £102, was a special favourite.

FABERGÉ
Samoyed "Jacko" *c.* 1907
Chalcedony, rose diamonds
h. 46 x w. 52 x d. 15 mm
ROYAL COLLECTION TRUST

On his return from the 1895–8 Jackson-Harmsworth Expedition to Franz Josef Land in the Arctic, Major Frederick G. Jackson presented Alexandra with a Samoyed named Jacko, which had helped pull the sledges.

The dog's hospital from *The Lady's Realm* 1901

The kennels were duly inspected and each was found to consist of an inner sleeping compartment, with an iron bedstead and straw mattress, which was well-ventilated, 'with good sanitary arrangements' and whitewashed once a year. The sleeping area led to a 'sitting-room' supplied with straw and fresh water. Iron gates enclosed each kennel from the central yard, and 'good grass' ran alongside. And then to the inmates, as Sarah Tooley described them:

> *I first made the acquaintance of a handsome Siberian sledge-dog, with a white body and black head. He had for companion a little fox-terrier. The contrast was amusing, for they appeared a perfect David and Jonathan together. The next kennels displayed two rough-coated collies and a lovely white Samoyed sledge-dog hailing from the Arctic regions. He had a sweet face which bespoke good-temper, and came in a friendly way to his gate, jumping up in great excitement and poking his nose through the rails ...*
>
> *The famous collies, 'Sandringham Nicety' and 'Newmarket Tip'...next claimed my attention, and from these I passed to the admiration of three lovely deerhound puppies bred at Sandringham. Near by was the home of 'Collie Lochiel', commonly called 'Locky'...He is a very great pet, and frequently walks with Her Majesty. I should say that she endeavours to give most of the dogs that pleasure in turn, and names those whom she may wish to accompany her. Sometimes the Queen takes eight or ten dogs out with her at one time.*
>
> *Another dog of special interest was a St Bernard, with a lovely face and head. She is the daughter of 'Leo', the famous begging-dog at the Cork Hospital. In the next kennel was 'Borezoi' [sic – most probably Vassilka] a wolfhound sent from Russia by the Dowager-Empress. It had a beautiful white silky coat, marked with fawn on the head and side. 'Come along boy,' says Mr Brundson, approaching another kennel; and out comes 'Alex' the well-known Russian dog... and champion prize-winner, there being a hundred first and special, seven champions, and six premiers to his credit. He has been painted by Miss Maud Earl, several times photographed with the Queen, and is the most widely known of the Sandringham pets ...*
>
> *Passing by other dogs less noticeable, I was amused by the antics of a little company of Clumber spaniel puppies, home-bred and the progeny of the King's dog. Then there were a number of Dachshunds and Spitz dogs, of which the Queen is very fond; and Bassets, rough and smooth, are a speciality at Sandringham. 'Saraceneska' (usually called 'Nesca'), the mother of the smooth Bassets, and 'Vivian', a rough hound, have been prize-winners, and so also has 'Nesca's' son, 'Lockey'; but the most noted amongst the Bassets are 'Sandringham Babel' and 'Sandringham Bobs', who have been victors in many competitions. Next I was greeted by a famous blood-hound, used for hare-hunting; and three saucy fox-terriers jumped to the gate of their kennel in great excitement.*
>
> *Crossing to the other side of the enclosure, I made the acquaintance of 'Schipperk', sent to Queen Alexandra by the King of the Belgians, and Princess Victoria's black poodle, 'Gyp', a very handsome dog. At present the Princess Victoria's favourite pet, whom she takes everywhere with her, is a white Maltese named 'Fluffy'. A noisy little dog was the fox-terrier 'Swift', to whom I was next introduced. He was given to the Queen in Denmark. Next I came to 'Wrangler', a very friendly dog, who shook hands repeatedly and seemed loth to part. He... kept up a constant charm of noise while I was making friends with the King's French bulldogs and a little black pug. 'Heather', the Prince of Wales's companion dog, who had been left in Mr Brundson's care while the Prince was away, looked as though he did not approve of Colonial visits.*

Happily, in the dogs' hospital the lady journalist found 'only one patient, and he did not look very ill'. In the kitchen, lined with portraits of canine celebrities, she inspected oatmeal mash and broth made from bullocks' and sheep's heads, boiling in coppers for four o'clock

Alexandra with lapdog, 1902
Postcard
PRIVATE COLLECTION, SUFFOLK

servings. Sacks of biscuits stood in an adjacent larder, beside the mill for grinding them. As well as a 'simple and nutritive' diet, the dogs were exercised for specific durations, depending on their size, and all were regularly washed in a big bath. The visitor added:

> *Old favourites live out their lives in peace, and when they die are buried in a little graveyard set apart near the kennels, and a tombstone is erected to their memory. I noticed the grave of 'Sam', a brown poodle, for many years the companion of the Princess Victoria, who used to have the clippings of his coat spun into yarn for crocheting shawls. He died in 1900. There, too, was the grave of the Duke of Clarence's old favourite, 'Venus', who had been taken to be the King's dog. 'Venus' was greatly beloved by all the Royal family for Prince 'Eddy's' sake, and his death last March was a great grief to the King and Queen.*

The visit ended in the Queen's stables, and this part of the tour might have taken an entire morning in itself. For Alexandra, it was noted, toured the estate each day in a pony and trap (in preference to a tricycle and to newfangled motor cars), rode regularly on different mounts and was driven to church and the railway station with separate pairs of horses chosen for the specific task (the more sedate being entrusted with the clerical mission). And for the royal children there was both a donkey and a zebra. Sarah Tooley's invaluable record opens:

> *The Queen's stables, which are not far from the kennels, were specially built for her ponies in 1879. They have a picturesque appearance with the clock-tower over the gateway, and are ranged round a great square courtyard, harness-horses to the right and saddle-horses to the left. The stables are lofty, with excellent sanitation; the walls are lined with white glazed tiles. The stalls look very smart engraved with the Royal coat-of-arms and with brass mounts on the pillars. There are bars to pull out at night across the stalls for the better protection of the horses. Above each manger is the name of the horse in gold on a tablet of red and blue. So dainty and neat is everything about the Queen's stables that even the litter on the floor has a plaited fringe of straw.*
>
> *The Queen names her own horses, and practically makes pets of all of them, not simply her special saddle-horses. They know her voice and footstep, and eagerly turn their heads as she approaches the stalls. She always visits them at least once a week, and feeds them with carrots and apples. Her favourite horses are bay, and she likes them to have tan harnesses with brass mounts.*

Sarah Tooley was introduced to Puffy and Mite, tandem bays used to drive a wicker cart, and three light-grey Hungarian horses (Hungary, Austria and Liechenstein), which the Queen drove in pairs. Greys Cromer, Bright and Brisk and chestnuts Faithful Boy and Margate Buoy were used for short journeys in Norfolk, London and Windsor. Next came Battle, a veteran retired from active service; Yvonne, the favourite pony of Princess Maud; and Bator and Csllig, aged survivors of the four Hungarian ponies given to Alix by Bertie in 1875 as consolation gifts for not being allowed to join him on his Indian tour. Then there were Palmer, Tuck, Traveller and Benton, the quiet quartet entrusted with Sunday missions; and the inaptly named Deacon, collared and

Alexandra in carriage with children and dogs at Sandringham
PRIVATE COLLECTION

barred in his stall after savaging former companions such as Scot, Palmistry and Shahzada (the last of these bred at the Sandringham Stud and named after a visiting Shah of Persia). The inspection continued with phaeton driving-ponies Merry Antics, Belle, Bena and Beau – the last pair fitted with false tails to improve their appearance when in harness; and moved on to a new pony called Violet, Princess Victoria's horses Empress and Pompon, Marky – the Queen's favourite hack, her Arab horse Stamboul, Boxer, Betty, Bruiser, the black cob Newmarket, Louvima (named after Princesses Louise, Victoria and Maud), the King's buggy horse Tooting, and Wasp and Vivandiere, dear to the late Duke of Clarence. That made for an equine herd of 39 animals – plus the donkey and the zebra. All this in addition to the King's stud at Wolferton and Sandringham, where unnumbered thoroughbreds were in the care of the stud groom, Mr Walker.

In the harness room of the Queen's stables, beside a display of brown saddles and 'dainty riding-whips mounted with gold', there were reminders of the dear departed – the hooves of some, and the ears and forelock of Viva, the Queen's favourite riding hack. Sarah Tooley also paid her respects at the former stall of 'faithful' Huffy:

> *Huffy' was a special pet with the Queen, who used to drive him about the villages in the Blues cart when visiting the cottages. It was 'Huffy's' happy privilege to be the bearer of gifts to old and young, and the children saw him coming along the lanes with delight, for well they knew that there were oranges in the cart-box; and the old folks brightened when he drew up at their doors, knowing that he carried tea and sugar or the Christmas present of a warm shawl . . .*

FABERGÉ
Donkey *c.* 1907
Chalcedony, rose Diamonds
h. 26 x w. 33 x d. 12 mm
ROYAL COLLECTION TRUST

On her 1907 visit to Sandringham, the Dowager Russian Empress was snapped feeding a donkey. This may have been Maria, seen in 1901 pulling the younger princes and princesses on carriage drives, and looking 'very smart in a wonderful red and gold harness'. George V bought this model from Fabergé's London shop on 7 November 1910 for £11 5s. His four purchases that day – also including a French bulldog and a box with a view of Sandringham on the lid (both featured in this book and exhibition) – cost £168 10s, after a 10 per cent royal discount.

Alfred Munnings
1878–1959
Sunny June 1901
Oil on canvas
h. 765 x w. 1280 mm
NORWICH CASTLE MUSEUM AND ART GALLERY

Alfred Munnings was a Waveney miller's son and brilliant impressionistic painter of horse-rife East Anglia. Here a Norfolk farmworker leads a mare and her foal through a meadow sparkling with wildflowers in the first summer of the Edwardian age.

This shire stallion (right) is traditionally identified as Field Marshal, one of several champion working horses on the Sandringham estate in 1907. But it may show fellow prize-winner Hoe Forest King.

On 30 June 1894 the *Norwich Mercury* reported on the second biennial sale of Hackneys and Harness Horses from the Royal Stud at Wolferton. Two special trains were scheduled from London and Cambridge, and the Sandringham house-party entertained to lunch in a huge marquee on the lawn included Nicholas, the Russian Tsarevich. The news item continued:

Before commencing the sale Mr Somerville Tattersall said he wished to point out that one of the sires of the stud was the celebrated horse Field Marshal, which had just been paraded in the ring, and that many of the lots about to be offered were the progeny of that horse, which had been winning so many prizes lately.

Fifty brood mares, fillies, harness horses and hacks fetched a total of £6,652 10s. One mare, Eileen, together with her bay filly foal, Field of Erin, by Field Marshal, returned with Nicholas to Russia after a winning bid of 170 guineas (£178 10s).

FABERGÉ
Field Marshal *c.* 1907
Aventurine quartz, cabochon sapphires
h. 145 x w. 170 x d. 57 mm
ROYAL COLLECTION TRUST

FABERGÉ
Iron Duke *c.* 1907
Aventurine quartz, cabochon sapphires, nephrite, silver-gilt
h. 105 x w. 138 x d. 54 mm
ROYAL COLLECTION TRUST

Iron Duke was Edward VII's shooting pony. This Sandringham sculpture was bought by Queen Alexandra from Fabergé's London branch in December 1909, for £70. It was presumably a present for what turned out to the King's last Christmas.

At Sandringham the Fabergé sculptors made a series of progressively smaller models in wax, adjusting for visual accuracy, Once those minor changes required by the King had been completed, the fragile models were carefully packed and sent to St Petersburg for rendering first in plaster and finally in hardstones, precious metals, gems and enamels. Persimmon and the borzoi dog Vassilka went to the firm's silversmiths in Moscow, as their legs were too slender for stone. Fabergé himself closely supervised production – indeed, the scope and stature of the Sandringham commission may have prompted the 1908 opening of a stone-carving workshop in the St Petersburg premises. Previously, stone had been cut and shaped at the Woerffel works elsewhere in the Russian capital, or in the Stern works at Oberstein in Germany. And so, with greater ease, the director was able to select stones to depict not merely a particular species, but an individual in a living moment (hence variegated agate for Pekingese and poodle, jasper for black cat and Norfolk black turkey, aventurine quartz for chestnut horses and pink pigs, chalcedony for fawn Jersey bull, grey mice and gold-coated and white-shirted dormouse). As quoted by Bainbridge, King Edward's 'stock command' during the Norfolk operation had been: 'We must not make any duplicates.' The unique bodies of the Sandringham menagerie were most probably carved by the Russians Kremlev and Derbyshev, both of whom had studied at Ekaterinburg Art School, at the centre of the Siberian mining industry for multicoloured hardstones, such as the dark-grey or black volcanic glass obsidian, dark-green nephrite jade and lapis lazuli – a deep-blue stone flecked with gold.

FABERGÉ
Pekingese 1907
Agate, rose diamonds
h. 36 x w. 44 x d. 19 mm
ROYAL COLLECTION TRUST

The first Pekingese in Britain was the unfortunately named Looty, brought from China after the Second Opium War and given to Queen Victoria in 1861. Alexandra loved these dogs, along with other exotic small breeds. In 1905 the Empress of Japan sent her eight Pekingese, but seven died on the journey.

FABERGÉ
Poodle *c.* 1907
Agate, crystal
h. 65 x w. 78 x d. 27 mm
ROYAL COLLECTION TRUST

FABERGÉ
Jersey Bull *c.* 1907
Chalcedony, cabochon rubies
h. 38 x w. 62 x d. 31 mm
ROYAL COLLECTION TRUST

Sandringham's herds of prized pedigree cattle included shorthorns, red polls, Irish Dexters and Jerseys. In July 1902, *Country Life* reported that Alexandra was often to be seen

making a progress through the cowhouse, patting and talking to her special favourites among the Jerseys, and rewarding them with a basket of carrots carried for the purpose. The exquisite kindness which permeates all she does of course finds constant expression in her love of animals.

The hardstone animal carvings were then passed to the workshop of the head workmaster – by this point Henrik Wigström, Fabergé's third and final chief craftsman. Here they were polished and adorned with any gold fittings, such as the feet of the birds, and the straws on which *Queen Alexandra's Dormouse* nibbles beneath its whiskers of newly discovered platinum. Then the gem-set eyes and ears were added, along with any enamelled features. Only one Sandringham-associated animal, the goose with outstretched neck, has been positively identified in what remain of the Wigström design albums.

Once completed, and approved by Fabergé, the animals were sent in small batches to the London branch, where they were purchased over nearly a decade by the royal family and their friends. Bertie and Alix were supposed to have first approval of the choicest new arrivals, with previews at Buckingham Palace, but there seems to have been something of a scramble at times, for so finite a supply. The problem had been foreseen by Minny. In 1906 she wrote to Alix, 'Now that silly Fabergé has his shop in London, you have everything, and I cannot send anything new, so I am furious.'

The most celebrated Sandringham carving – of Bertie's favourite dog, Caesar – was never to be owned by him. It was bought by the Honourable Mrs Greville on 29 November 1910 (for £35) as a gift for the widowed Alix. Perhaps its late arrival was due to the fact that the Norfolk terrier's worldwide celebrity (and notoriety) arose when he followed after the King's coffin in the funeral procession. Maybe such fame spurred Fabergé to take out a wax maquette made three years earlier, and belatedly oversee the making of a kingly model.

FABERGÉ
Workmaster Henrik Wigström
Goose 1911
Quartzite, obsidian, rose diamonds, gold
h. 30 x w. 70 x d. 23 mm
ROYAL COLLECTION TRUST

This is the only Sandringham-linked Fabergé model known in a workmaster's design book. The page of Wigström watercolour images is reproduced courtesy of A La Vieille Russie, New York.

FABERGÉ
Mouse model
Plaster
l. 51 x h. 38 mm
A LA VIEILLE RUSSIE, NEW YORK

In the production process for Fabergé animals, plaster maquettes came between initial wax models and final renderings in gems, precious metals and hardstones. This example is a very rare survival.

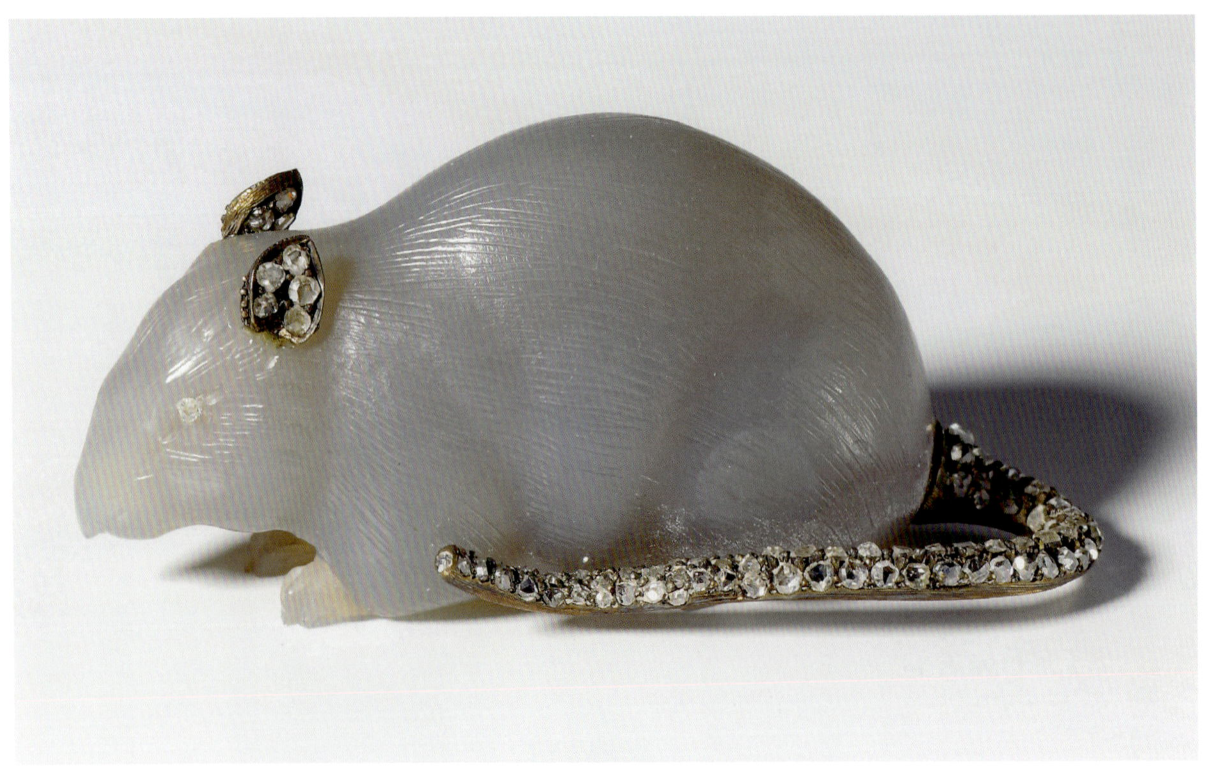

FABERGÉ
Rat *c.* 1907
Chalcedony, rose diamonds, silver
h. 22 x w. 46 x d. 20 mm
ROYAL COLLECTION TRUST

Across England by the 18th century the brown rat displaced the black rat, which had probably spread bubonic plague via infected fleas. The final outbreak was in Suffolk from December 1906 – with the last of 16 fatalities in June 1918. By then fancy rats had been bred, from unusually coloured brown rats, as pets.

FABERGÉ
Mouse *c.* 1907
Chalcedony, rose diamonds, silver
h. 32 x w. 54 x d. 30 mm
ROYAL COLLECTION TRUST

Eight Fabergé rats and mice, now in the Royal Collection, mostly comprise highly realistic hardstone bodies adorned with diamond-encrusted eyes, ears and tails – turning nature into a fabulous joke.

Much as she cherished her works by Fabergé, the ever-generous Alix included some of them among the items she presented to a circle of friends as mementoes of her late husband. Certain gifts were returned to senders – the most spectacular being the Art Nouveau cigarette case made in blue guilloché enamel entwined with a diamond-encrusted snake given to the King by Mrs Keppel after the Sandringham commission, and perhaps as a token of it. The snake biting its own tail symbolises eternal love. Alice Keppel in turn would give it to Queen Mary in 1936, following the death of George V. The case still contains the stub of one of Bertie's cigars.

Alix's readiness to part with some of her best pieces of Fabergé may also suggest that she viewed them as charming decorative items rather than major works of art. Even she – for whom a courtier had to be discreetly charged with retrieving overly generous presents – wouldn't have given away a Titian. And so the model of the smooth-haired basset hound, *Sandringham Dido*, a star among the 1907 canine sitters since winning Best of Breed at Crufts that year, entered the Royal Collection in 1912 and then left it at some uncertain point. The whereabouts of the ruby-eyed model in white magnesite are now unknown.

FABERGÉ
Queen Alexandra's Dormouse *c.* 1910
Chalcedony, platinum, gold, sapphires
h. 62 x w. 52 x d. 58 mm
ROYAL COLLECTION TRUST

There was a table set out under a tree in front of the house, and the March Hare and the Hatter were having tea at it: a Dormouse was sitting between them, fast asleep, and the other two were using it as a cushion, resting their elbows on it, and talking over its head. 'Very uncomfortable for the Dormouse,' thought Alice; 'only, as it's asleep, I suppose it doesn't mind.'

So begins Chapter 7, 'A Mad Tea-Party', in *Alice's Adventures in Wonderland*, by Lewis Carroll (pen name of mathematician Charles Lutwidge Dodgson), first published in 1865 and in print ever since. The instant popularity of the story, illustrated by Sir John Tenniel, swept through the British royal family (a delighted Queen Victoria being blissfully oblivious to rumours that the tempestuous Queen of Hearts was a caricature of her) and also affected the young Oscar Wilde. According to Henry Bainbridge, Fabergé modelled both Alice and the Mad Hatter.

The hazel or common dormouse – the only dormouse species native to Britain – weaves nests of shredded honeysuckle bark, leaves and grasses in hedges linked to woodland. It hibernates from October to May and saves energy with spells of curled-up torpor at other times. However, since the First World War a drastic loss of hedgerows across Britain – where more than 1,500 insect species have been recorded – has been especially severe in East Anglia. As a result, the dormouse is now scarce in the eastern counties.

The gentle nature of the dormouse, as well as the consummate quality of its depiction, led to this model alone being named as Queen Alexandra's own. Alix bought it in 1912. The purchase price of £33 was the same as a first-class berth on the Titanic.

FABERGÉ
Workmaster Henrik Wigström
Norfolk Black Turkey *c.* 1908
Obsidian, lapis lazuli, purpurine, rose diamonds, gold
h. 97 x w. 85 x d. 73 mm
ROYAL COLLECTION TRUST

So focused were the Fabergé craftsmen and jewellers on creating individual pieces that bizarre disparities of scale had resulted. This bothered Alix not a bit. From gifts and her own purchases, her Fabergé pieces – outshone only by those of her sister, Tsaritsa Alexandra Feodorovna and Grand Duchess Maria Pavlovna – came to be crammed together. As Lord Knutsford, visiting Sandringham House on Alix's birthday, 1 December 1909 (her last as Queen), noted:

> *I never saw anything like them, over 100, and some most beautiful things. The Queen likes most agate animals, of which she has a magnificent collection in two large glass cabinets in the drawing room, which every evening are lit up by electricity.*

New arrivals that day included *Norfolk Black Turkey* and the ruby-eyed Clumber spaniel *Sandringham Lucy* – both gifts from the Prince of Wales, who would be George V six months later. The pair had cost him a princely £157 (but he could claim a filial right to break his mother's injunction on any gift – including any work by Fabergé – costing more than £50).

Along with the flowers that also remained redolent of the atmosphere of Sandringham, the animals would be Alix's favourite Fabergé works to the last. And to this day, after a further three generations have swollen the Royal Collection's holding of Fabergé to 570 pieces, they retain a distinct appeal. As Sir Sacheverell Sitwell wrote in the catalogue for a Queen Elizabeth II Coronation Exhibition of Fabergé, staged by Wartski in 1953: 'These particular Fabergé objects are of no tragic significance at all, which makes them all the more delightful.'

FABERGÉ
Snail *c.* 1910
Chalcedony, jasper
h. 45 x w. 100 x d. 37 mm
ROYAL COLLECTION TRUST

If this is a Sandringham snail, it is the only Norfolk animal rendered by Fabergé at life-size. It's certainly a beautiful example of 'mosaic sculpture', where hardstones have been carved and polished for textural contrast – here evoking both the hard, shiny surface of the shell and the soft flesh.

CHAPTER ELEVEN

The Bet

As Edward VII's most successful racehorse, Persimmon was the only animal to win multiple Sandringham commission tributes. Sculptor Boris Frödman-Cluzel made the wax model from which a silver statuette was produced by Henrik Wigström in 1908, on a base of green nephrite to simulate turf. Six bronze versions were later cast as gifts. The mark of the same workmaster was added to a frame for a photograph of the champion horse, sporting Bertie's racing colours in red and blue guilloché enamels garlanded with gold, silver-gilt and moonstones.

Persimmon won the Derby, St Leger and Jockey Stakes at Newmarket in 1896, and the Ascot Gold Cup and Eclipse Stakes the following year. His prize money funded Sandringham's 8-acre (3.2-hectare) Walled Garden, with teak glasshouses – supplying fruit, flowers and vegetables for the house – dubbed the Persimmon range.

The Derby victory came on 3 June 1896 – Prince George's 31st birthday – against the odds, and over the favourite St Frusquin, owned by Leopold de Rothschild. Behind for most of the race, Persimmon finally won by a neck, to set a new course record. George wrote in his

Unknown Maker
Persimmon horseshoe trophy 1896
Iron, gilt, fabric, wood
h. 350 x w. 290 x d. 50 mm
PRIVATE COLLECTION

diary: 'Papa led Persimmon in, he got a tremendous ovation. I never saw such a sight & I never heard such cheering. I won £300 on the race.'

Queen Victoria told her youngest daughter Beatrice: 'Bertie has won the Derby. I cannot rejoice as I know what dear Papa felt & as it sets an example to so many who get ruined and break their Parents' hearts. Of course I congratulated him.'

Persimmon, a four-time champion sire, did not long outlive the Fabergé commission. In 1908 he suffered a fractured pelvis when falling in his box, and had to be put down. His stuffed head and tail are now on loan from the Royal Collection to the National Horseracing Museum at Newmarket. As a birthday gift in 1905 his owner had received, from fellow members of the Jockey Club, a life-size statue by Adrian Jones, which still stands on the lawn of the Sandringham Stud where the champion was born in 1893, from a mare called Perdita II and the famous racehorse St Simon. His brothers Florizel (born 1891) and Diamond Jubilee (born 1897) helped swell the total winnings to more than £70,000 (£4 million today) – but half that royal bag was Persimmon's.

Bertie's other race victors included Ambush II, winner of the Grand National in 1900. Minoru won the 1909 Derby, and on 6 May 1910 – the day Edward VII died – his bay filly, Witch of the Air, triumphed in the Spring Plate at Kempton Park. News reached the dying monarch just in time and he said: 'I am very glad.'

Princess Alexandra
Persimmon and Groom at Sandringham 1900
Photograph
PRIVATE COLLECTION

FABERGÉ
Workmaster Henrik Wigström
Frame with a photograph of Persimmon *c.* 1908
Gelatin silver print, two-colour gold, guilloché red and blue enamel, moonstones, silver-gilt
h. 120 x w. 158 x d. 101 mm
ROYAL COLLECTION TRUST

FABERGÉ
Workmaster Henrik Wigström
Persimmon 1908
Silver, nephrite
h. 243 x w. 312 x d. 96 mm
ROYAL COLLECTION TRUST

CHAPTER TWELVE

Gone Astray

When the King's Irish terrier, Jack, died in 1903, the Duchess of Newcastle gave him a Norfolk terrier. Caesar soon became a favourite – present at the inspection of Fabergé wax models, which included his own likeness in chalcedony, with ruby eyes and a collar in gold and enamel bearing the legend 'I BELONG TO THE KING'.

As the years advanced, Caesar remained a boisterous puppy. He barked, snapped and 'worried' the trousers of gentlemen striving for decorum in the presence of the King. Cue roars of royal laughter. George Stamper, the chauffeur and motor mechanic who took monarch and mutt on long drives in Norfolk and elsewhere, recalled outings on which Caesar would inevitably misbehave. He said the King would shake his stick at him and say very slowly: "You naughty dog. You naughty, naughty dog." Caesar would wag his tail and "smile" cheerfully up into this master's eyes, until His Majesty smiled back in spite of himself.

The wire-haired terrier was taken to France and Germany, and at the Bohemian spa of Marienbad in August 1907 Caesar suddenly fell ill. This prompted such alarm that a vet costing £200 a day was nearly summoned from London, before Vienna supplied a cheaper solution. The patient recovered and returned to Sandringham to sit for a Fabergé modeller.

Caesar was a wild symbol for his wayward master's successful reign. The man deemed by his mother constitutionally unfit for kingship had a coronation delayed by near-fatal appendicitis. But he was far more suited to the role of a modern monarch than she had ever been. With the diplomat's gift of seeing both sides, the King was able to mediate in Liberal–Tory political and constitutional battles. He had been a pall-bearer at the funeral of William Gladstone, the veteran Liberal premier whom Victoria had loathed, and had sought to introduce old-age pensions at his first State Opening of Parliament. All those travels to foreign fleshpots and watering holes had made 'Edward the Caresser' the perfect peacemaker. He spoke fluent French and

Caesar 1910
Postcards
PRIVATE COLLECTION, SUFFOLK

FABERGÉ
Caesar *c.* 1908
Chalcedony, gold, enamel, rubies
h. 59 x w. 84 x d. 33 mm
ROYAL COLLECTION TRUST

Where's Master? 1910
Book
h. 190 x w. 130 x d. 15 mm
PRIVATE COLLECTION, SUFFOLK

German; the Entente Cordiale was his initiative, and this Uncle of Europe fully agreed with his wife in wanting closer ties with Russia.

Caesar's antics were devoured in the press of a dog-loving nation, and indeed across an empire. His portrait featured on popular postcards and on the lid of a children's board game designed in his honour, in which he played havoc with a scatter of cats. When the King died, Caesar was said to wander the corridors of Buckingham Palace in search of his master. A saga of dogged devotion was perpetuated when the Norfolk terrier, led by a Highlander, walked immediately after the coffin on Alexandra's instructions – the crowned heads of Europe, including an enraged Kaiser Wilhelm, following on behind. In 1901 Wilhelm's grandmother, Queen Victoria, had died in his arms. In 1910, after nine years of rising personal and national rivalry, he processed to his uncle's funeral service with a view of a dog's bottom. The Kaiser's emotions had always been deeply conflicted, and his actions erratic. Now, with a supreme sense of self-importance greatly offended, his hatred of Britain hardened.

Bertie's funeral – with twice the crowd that came out to mourn Victoria – saw an outpouring of public sympathy for his dog. More tribute postcards were printed in huge quantities, and in Germany the Steiff family of toy-makers, inventors of the teddy bear in 1902, caught the mood – and the market – with a model Caesar. A portrait study by Maud Earl, entitled Silent Sorrow, was published in the *Illustrated London News* a fortnight after the King's death; and a book, *Where's Master?*, purporting to have been penned by Caesar himself, was hurriedly printed – and reprinted. Over more than a score of editions, the volume sold in excess of 100,000 copies and became the runaway best-seller of 1910.

Alix was often said to have loved all dogs. But despite the funereal theatrics she had stage-managed, she may have made an exception of Caesar. When a visiting Margot Asquith, wife of the then Prime Minister, remarked on Caesar's devotion, the Dowager Queen responded: 'Horrid little dog! He never went near my poor husband when he was ill!' Margot then mentioned that her spouse had seen the pet lying at the dead King's feet. 'For warmth, my dear,' Alix replied. Such antipathy may have aided a story that when the dowager was sending key possessions to Bertie's friends as souvenirs, Caesar was dispatched to Lillie Langtry. In fact, she came to love the King's favourite dog in the early years of her widowhood and, when he died, in the fateful year of 1914, had him buried in the cemetery for very special pets in the grounds of Marlborough House. And Caesar, in sculpted marble, now sits at the feet of the King on his tomb in St George's Chapel, Windsor.

Sadly, a peacemaker's legacy is not set in stone. Friendships also foster fiendships. Little more than four years after Bertie's funeral, the world exploded. As W.C. Sellar and R.J. Yeatman joked in *1066 and All That: A Memorable History of England*, published in 1930: 'Edward VII smoked cigars, was addicted to entente cordials . . . and invented appendicitis . . . King Edward's new policy of peace was very successful and culminated in the Great War to End War.'

Royal mourners at the funeral of Edward VII 1910

Postcard

PRIVATE COLLECTION, SUFFOLK

CHAPTER THIRTEEN

A Woman's Kingdom

For all the palaces in which their formal lives were played out, Alix and Minny loved more modest retreats. From 1906 they shared the substantial villa of Hvidøre, on the coast north of Copenhagen, for their frequent visits to their home country. And on their later reunions in Norfolk, as well as picnicking in the Model Dairy, they could imagine themselves as fishermen's wives in what was known as the Queen's Bungalow, on the shingle bank at Snettisham.

Designed by the Norwich architect C.S. Beck, as were other follies in and around Sandringham, the cottage was built of tile, timber and local carrstone. With an upturned boat for an entrance porch, it seemed to have been vaguely inspired by the beached houseboat Charles Dickens had seen at Great Yarmouth and transformed into Peggotty's cottage in David Copperfield. The roofline of this Arts and Crafts curiosity was pierced with the legend 'NISI DOMINUS A R I MCMVIII' ('Unless the Lord [builds the house, the builders labour in vain] Alexandra Regina Imperatrice 1908'). And leaning out into the sea air, as if on the prow of a Viking longboat, there was a carved dragon.

The northward view brought comforting memories of Denmark. And at low tide, when the sea had all but vanished, the sisters might have thought they were still on the edge of Doggerland around 6500 BC and could walk safely home to Jutland while barely getting their boots wet.

This escapist dream, which also resembled a Russian dacha, was demolished in 1925, the year of Alix's death, and the materials were used to build nearby Shernborne village hall. Had it lingered, the cottage would have been smashed to pulp and swept away in the Great Floods of 1953.

Queen Alexandra's Bungalow *c.* 1908
Postcard
PRIVATE COLLECTION, SUFFOLK

The enamelled and bejewelled hardstone Fabergé handle to this stylish sunshade was pleasantly cool in the hand.

British manufacture
Parasol *c.* 1900
Silk with chenile fringe
l. 650 x w. 330 x d. 60 mm
VICTORIA AND ALBERT MUSEUM. GIVEN BY LADY HELEN NUTTING (1890–1973)

FABERGÉ
Workmaster Mikhail Perkhin
Parasol handle 1896–1903
Bowenite pommel with enamelled gold collar set with diamonds
VICTORIA AND ALBERT MUSEUM. GIVEN BY LADY HELEN NUTTING (1890–1973)

Maison Laferrière
Designer Madeleine Laferrière (1847–1912)
Evening dress *c.* 1900
Silk satin bodice and skirt
l. 1070 mm
VICTORIA AND ALBERT MUSEUM. GIVEN BY LADY LLOYD

This elegant evening dress was designed by the famous Paris fashion house Maison Laferrière. It was worn by Alexandra, who was considered to dress with exemplary taste.

CHAPTER FOURTEEN

An Adventure

Another word for Sandringham in the long era of Bertie and Alix might have been 'Beckland' – for no fewer than 31 members of the Beck family were born or lived on the Norfolk estate until the clan connection began to break in 1936, during the brief reign of Edward VIII.

In 1865 farmer, land agent and auctioneer Edmund Beck – from a pioneering family of land-improvers in Norfolk – was appointed to run the Sandringham estate and make it a model enterprise, with the winning of prizes at agricultural shows at home and abroad part of the plan. In 1880 his second son, Frank, became his assistant, also helping to administer the Royal Stud. With the Prince's trainer, John Porter, Frank selected a mare called Perdita II, which had a foal called Persimmon. Frank married Mary Plumpton Wilson, of West Newton, in 1891 – the year Edmund Beck died after a carriage accident at the gates of York Cottage. The heredity principle enjoyed by royalty could also apply to Sandringham staff and, at the age of 30, Frank Beck duly followed his father as land agent. Like that of Edward VII, the reign of Frank Beck was a signal success – assisted occasionally by his younger brother, Arthur, who would eventually succeed him. In the 1901 Coronation honours the new King awarded his land agent membership of the Royal Victorian Order. A knighthood from King Haakon of Norway followed five years later.

As well as overseeing the estate and enhancing its reputation, Frank Beck ensured the comfort of a constant flow of guests who were met in carriages or cars at Wolferton railway station and delivered back again. The parties included Russian tsars and tsaritsas, German emperors and empresses, a score of other crowned heads and a small army of European princes and princesses. Plus all the courtiers, politicians, military officers, diplomats and sundry figures across the spectrum of public life who were invited to Sandringham.

Frank and Mary Beck had six children: five daughters, and a son who died in infancy and is buried in Sandringham churchyard. In January 1907 the family's Visitors Book was signed with accompanying messages by Queen Alexandra and the Dowager Empress of Russia, and that year Frank oversaw the arrangements for Fabergé's Sandringham commission. He found the sculptors studio space and lodgings. By the end of the project he and Mary had learned that a friendship between their eldest daughter Margaretta (Meg) and the visiting Nicholas Fabergé had taken a romantic turn, and further contact between the two was forbidden.

Frank Beck
Photograph
PRIVATE COLLECTION

Frank Beck was a close colleague and friend of General Sir Dighton Probyn, one of British history's most colourful characters. Probyn had joined the Bengal Army at 16, and a decade later was a veteran of the 1857–9 Indian Mutiny, for which he received a Victoria Cross for multiple acts of 'gallantry and daring'. This emblem of British imperialism cut an especially dashing figure in Indian dress. As such, he became a pin-up for all the contradictions of the Victorian age. Bertie made Sir Dighton an equerry in 1872, a decade before he retired from the army – but honours continued to come thick and fast. He was rewarded with a sinecure court position, before courageously accepting a role as Secretary to the Prince of Wales and Comptroller of the Household. His Herculean task was to keep the spendthrift Bertie and Alix solvent. Amazingly, thanks to Sir Dighton, and to background financiers, the Prince was in credit at the bank when he ascended to the throne in 1901.

Sir Dighton's wife Letitia died, at Sandringham, in the same month as Victoria, and he remained devoted to Alexandra as Queen and then as Dowager. His expertise remained essential. In later years he was bowed by age – and doubtless by the difficulties of his office – and a long white beard hid the VC he wore on ceremonial occasions. Alix carried a knife in his company, to cut open his shirt collar when he had seizures. A late photo in which she stands over a decrepit figure, hands on his shoulders, can be seen two ways. She is devoted to the servant whom she will not allow to leave. To him, she was 'The Blessed Lady'. Sir Dighton Probyn died, still in harness, at the age of 91 – at Sandringham in 1924.

Sir Dighton was delighted when Frank Beck, at the request of Edward VII, set up the Sandringham Company as part of a new Territorial Force – placing in military training many of the estate staff involved in the Fabergé commission. With rank dictated by social class, members of the local gentry like Frank Beck and his two nephews became the officers. The estate's foremen, butlers, head gamekeepers and head gardeners became the NCOs, while farm labourers, grooms and household servants comprised the rank and file. The Becks espoused values of chivalry and patriotism. Frank had won his school prize as the best example of a Christian gentleman, and nephew Alec had already served in the Boer War, taking his own horse, Bones, with him. When King Edward presented colours to several Norfolk volunteer units in Norwich in October 1909, the Sandringham Company

Sir Dighton Probyn as a young man in Indian dress *c.* 1860
Photograph
PRIVATE COLLECTION

Sir Dighton Probyn and Queen Alexandra 1922
Photograph
PRIVATE COLLECTION

was among them. Sir Dighton later won Alexandra's permission to pass on to Captain Beck a gold half-hunter fob watch that she had presented to him.

All the parades, manoeuvres and presentations of peacetime ended when the First World War began on 4 August 1914. The 5th Territorial Battalion Norfolk Regiment was mobilised that evening. The men assembled at East Dereham, before moving on to Colchester on 17 August. In November, Colonel Sir Horace Proctor Beauchamp, a cavalryman who had retired from the army in 1906, was appointed the 5th Norfolks' Commanding Officer. He had never served as an infantryman.

For a year, from February 1915, Allied forces were involved in the disastrous Dardanelles–Gallipoli campaign to take Constantinople, reopen Russian supply routes and launch a new eastern front. On 30 July the 5th Norfolks sailed from Liverpool on the liner Aquitania. At 54, Frank Beck need not have led his men to war, but was determined to do so. 'I formed them,' he said. 'How could I leave them now? The lads will expect me to go with them; besides, I promised their wives and children I would look after them.' In his absence, his younger brother, Arthur, became Sandringham land agent, having previously managed royal shooting rights on the neighbouring estate of Castle Rising and having conducted auctions of horses from the Wolferton Stud with Tattersall's. On a final home leave, Frank inscribed an album for his wife with the words 'You are with me for ever and all time – you are mine, I am yours. Frank, Sandringham July 21st 1915.'

The battalion reached Suvla Bay on 10 August, in the thick of the fighting. The climate veered from freezing to searing; many men already suffered from dysentery and the side-effects of inoculations and seasickness tablets; water was severely rationed. On 12 August – the Glorious Twelfth marking the start of the grouse-shooting season in upland Britain – the Norfolks were told they would attack that afternoon, with an advance over unknown territory in heat and daylight towards Turkish guns. They were cut down – like the cavalry in the Charge of the Light Brigade from the Crimean War, with which Colonel Beauchamp would have been more familiar. An order to fix bayonets pinpointed their positions as sunlight glinted on metal, just as it had on drawn sabres 61 years before. Frank Beck was last seen, by Private Dye of the Sandringhams, sitting under a tree with his

head on one side – exhausted, wounded or dead. He and many of the lads around him simply vanished into history and legend.

In his 1969 book *Akenfield: Portrait of an English Village*, Ronald Blythe presented a shocking image of rural life since the 1890s, from the perspective of the Suffolk village of Charsfield. Interviewees included a 71-year-old farm worker called Len Thompson, who, like the author's own father, had served at Gallipoli. The labourer recalled a terrible landing:

> *The first things we saw were big wrecked Turkish guns, the second a big marquee. It didn't make me think of the military but of the village fetes. Other people must have thought like this because I remember how we all rushed up to it, like boys getting into a circus, and then found it all laced up. We unlaced it and rushed in. It was full of corpses. Dead Englishmen, lines and lines of them, and with their eyes wide open. We all stopped talking. I'd never seen a dead man before and here I was looking at two or three hundred of them. It was our first fear. Nobody had mentioned this. I was very shocked. I thought of Suffolk and it seemed a happy place for the first time.*

Frank Beck
1861–1915
Sandringham Company of the Norfolk Regiment 1912
Photograph
LYNN MUSEUM

The biggest shock in the previous paragraph is, of course, the last sentence. It caused a sensation in 1969 – with one landed East Anglian reader buying the book at Liverpool Street Station and throwing it out of the train window before he reached Ipswich. He and others refused to believe that Suffolk or Norfolk had ever known such misery. And yet a widely imagined idyll came closest to reality at Sandringham.

Myth was added to mystery. In 1965, on the 50th anniversary of the Gallipoli Landings, a former sapper from New Zealand, supported by three other veterans, claimed to have seen the Norfolks advancing into a low-lying cloud, which then lifted to leave an empty scene. The smoke of war had thickened into a suggestion of divine intervention or abduction by aliens.

After the war ended, in November 1918, the War Graves Commission had searched the Gallipoli battlefields.

Frank Beck's medals 1910–1918
Metal, bronze, enamel
h. 250 x w. 220 x d. 40 mm
PRIVATE COLLECTION

Frank Beck memorial window, Church of Saint Peter and Saint Paul, West Newton

Of 36,000 Commonwealth servicemen who perished in the campaign, 13,000 lay in unidentified graves and another 14,000 bodies were never found. But the discovery of a Norfolk regimental cap badge was reported to the Reverend Charles Pierrepont Edwards, who was on a mission to find out the fate of the 5th Norfolks, almost certainly at the behest of Queen Alexandra. He explored the Suvla plain and recorded in his official report that in an area of one square mile (2.59 square kilometres), he identified 122 bodies as Norfolk men, from their shoulder titles. A claim, from later conversation, that he found all the corpses had been shot in the head, has never been verified. But this, plus a proven Turkish reluctance to take prisoners on other occasions, inspired the controversial ending to the BBC film *All the King's Men* – directed by Julian Jarrold and starring David Jason as Frank Beck and Maggie Smith as Queen Alexandra – which was screened on Remembrance Day in 1999. The drama, beautifully shot in Sandringham and the Norfolk countryside, was inspired by the 1992 book *The Vanished Battalion* by Nigel McCrery, who also co-produced the film.

Numbers of the Sandringham dead had also escalated amid the general mystery and misconceptions. Seventy-seven names are recorded on the Sandringham War Memorial as casualties of the Great War, among whom 18 died at Suvla Bay on 12 August 1915. Of these, Alec Beck – Frank's nephew – was a land agent and farmer living in the South Norfolk village of Seething. Seventeen estate staff were sufficient to form only a single section of one platoon (and consider a context where the total number of First World War dead on all sides has been estimated at above 17 million). In all, 156 men from the 5th Norfolks died in that abortive August advance. Frank's second nephew, Evelyn, another Norfolk farmer, from East Tuddenham in Breckland, survived Suvla Bay. He was killed on 19 April 1917 in Gaza, on a deadly day when the toll among the 5th Norfolks reached a record 208 lives.

But it was faithful Frank Beck himself who was most mourned at Sandringham House, and prolonged investigations ordered by Alexandra and effected by Sir Dighton Probyn finally had a positive and poignant result. The watch from Alexandra via Sir Dighton, in Frank's pocket when he died, was discovered in post-war Smyrna (now Izmir). It was brought back to Sandringham in 1922, and presented to Meg Beck on her wedding day. This was the Meg who might have been Mrs Fabergé, and who had three queens (Alexandra, Mary and Maud) for godmothers. The tiny timepiece remains a treasured possession in the Beck family and enduring proof of the significance of small things.

Clark of Bond Street
Frank Beck's half-hunter watch *c.* 1910
Gold
h. 50 x w. 40 mm
PRIVATE COLLECTION

CHAPTER FIFTEEN

A Drama

In August 1914 Minny was staying with Alix at Sandringham. When they heard that war had been declared, Minny said, 'My life's work is complete.' The sisters had indeed striven for more than half a century to bring Britain and Russia together, and to break apart alliances with Germany. In February 1913 the Dowager Empress had been a key figure in vast ceremonial commemorations for 300 years of Romanov rule in Russia. It was to be said that the reigning family focused so much on the past because it was so fearful of the future. The point was horribly underlined the following month when Minny and Alix's favourite brother, King George of Greece, was assassinated in Salonika on the eve of celebrations for his Golden Jubilee. The family was shattered by those shots in the Balkans, but no new war was fostered and no kingdom fell. After the killing of Archduke Franz Ferdinand, Crown Prince of the Austro-Hungarian Empire, in Sarajevo 15 months later, all hell would break loose. In that lovely summer of 1914 Minny could have little idea of how her life – and that of all her Russian relatives, too – really was threatened with summary completion. Most immediately she suffered the inconvenience of being unable to return home by the normal central land route. Her train was halted at Berlin, and she was forced to travel via Denmark and Finland.

Not that Sandringham was wholly a safe haven. A suite of upper-storey rooms had been lost in an 1891 fire when preparations were under way for Bertie's birthday. And in 1903 Alix was awoken by her faithful attendant Charlotte Knollys when a fire was raging in the room above her bedroom. She escaped moments before the ceiling crashed down. Now, the fiery threat came from the skies.

Aerial bombing of British targets was approved by the Kaiser early in 1915, but London was exempted for fear of casualties among his royal kin (later, targets in the capital were allowed east of Charing Cross). On the night of 19–20 January 1915 the first Zeppelin airships were directed at industrial Humberside. Two blew off-course and drifted over Norfolk – one then killing two people in a raid on Great Yarmouth. The other caused havoc between Sheringham and King's Lynn, where it finally killed another two civilians. En route, bombs were dropped on Brancaster, Hunstanton, Heacham, Snettisham and, ironically in view of the injunction from Berlin, the Sandringham estate. Alexandra fully shared the fury of the media. She wrote to her old friend Admiral Lord Fisher – the naval reformer who had retired to Kilverstone Hall near Thetford in 1910, only to be recalled as First Sea Lord when war erupted (he resigned in 1915 over Winston Churchill's Gallipoli policy): 'Please let me have a lot of rockets with spikes or hooks on to defend our Norfolk coast. I am sure you could invent something of the sort which would bring down a few of those rascals.'

Alexandra and Maria Feodorovna in 1914

DAVID WILLIAM CRIPPS COLLECTION.

FABERGÉ
Workmaster Henrik Wigström
Crow *c.* 1907
Kalgan jasper, obsidian, aquamarine, silver-gilt
h. 78 x w. 157 x d. 57 mm
ROYAL COLLECTION TRUST

This hooded crow was bought by Queen Mary in November 1914, for £75. The First World War was under way, and Fabergé's London store would soon fall victim to the conflict. Hooded crows scavenged the 1914–18 killing fields from Flanders to Russia and Turkey. They were also winter migrants to Edwardian Norfolk, where they were called Kentish crows.

Gold-mounted emerald cabochon ring by Alexander Dementievich Ivanov (1908–1917) and enamel and gold open face-pocket watch by Pavel Buhre workshop, St Petersburg (*c.* 1900)
Watch: h. 67 x w. 43 x d. 10 mm; ring: h. 26 x w. 22 x d. 18 mm
PRIVATE COLLECTION, NORFOLK

Gamekeeper Esau Lewis joined the Norfolk Constabulary in 1876 and, over the next 44 years of police service, rose to be Deputy Chief Constable. While stationed at Dersingham, he was responsible for policing at Sandringham and received these tokens of appreciation from the Dowager Empress, probably during her visit in 1914.

On 17 September 1916 Alexandra wrote to her son:

> *We have been living through some gruesome moments here – just a fortnight ago we had those beastly Zepps over us. At 10 o'clock that Saturday evening they began. We were all sitting upstairs in Victoria's room when we suddenly were startled by the awful noise! And lo and behold, there was the awful monster over our heads. Everybody rushed up and wanted us to go downstairs. I must confess I was not a bit afraid – but it was a most uncanny feeling – poor Victoria was quite white in the face and horror-struck – but we all wanted to see it – the house was pitch black and at last Charlotte and I stumbled down in the darkness and found Colonel Davidson and Hawkins scrambling about outside so I also went out, but saw nothing and for the time the Zepps had flown but came back about four o'clock in the night and dropped bombs all over the place!!*

A propellor blade, subsequently believed to have been taken from a crashed Zeppelin but actually from

Charles John Holmes
1868–1936
Awaiting Zeppelins. Sandringham, January 1915
Oil on canvas
h. 690 x w. 765 mm
IMPERIAL WAR MUSEUM

Artist and National Portrait Gallery director Charles Holmes was part of an anti-aircraft gun crew at Sandringham. In 1919, when director of the National Gallery, he was commissioned to paint this scene from memory for the Imperial War Museum.

Zeppelin damage, St Peter's Plain, Great Yarmouth
Photograph
EASTERN DAILY PRESS

Zeppelin damage, Bentinck Street, King's Lynn
Photograph
EASTERN DAILY PRESS

a British plane, was kept as a trophy – like a tusk from some previously unknown animal shot on safari – and incorporated into a bizarre chair. Handed down through the Beck family, it is said to have been made at Sandringham's Carving School, though there was a wider fashion for such things at the time. Two technical schools had been set up for estate children by Alix when Princess of Wales, teaching woodwork/metalwork and needlework. Sister-in-law Vicky was so impressed, on a visit from Berlin, that she started a similar enterprise in Germany. After the First World War the Carving School, then under the wing of Queen Mary, took on wounded ex-servicemen. Regular exhibitions and sales of work were held, latterly in what is now Sandringham Museum. Furniture was also sold at Arts and Crafts exhibitions across the country and through London department stores. The Carving School closed in 1957.

Meanwhile in the depths of the First World War, the Dowager Queen, who spurned Sandringham economies at the best of times, was forced to consider painful measures in extremis. As she wrote:

> *It breaks my heart that this cruel, wicked, beastly war should be the cause of so many of my precious old friends my horses being slaughtered after all these years. My kennels and my dogs I will not have touched.*

Sandringham Carving School
Cake stand *c.* 1921
Wood
h. 970 x w. 280 mm
PRIVATE COLLECTION

Sandringham Carving School (?)
Chair with Bristol and Colonial propellor blade *c.* 1920
Wood
h. 1020 x w. 500 mm
PRIVATE COLLECTION

FABERGÉ
Workmaster Julius Rappoport
Model cannon *c.* 1900
Silver
l. 255 mm
ANDRE RUZHNIKOV

Several meticulously fashioned toy models of First World War cannons – with spring-loaded barrels and breach actions – were made for Tsarevich Alexei.

The Great War, which both sides had believed would end by Christmas 1914 in tremendous victory, had gone from bad to worse for everyone. Month on month and year on year, the casualty toll exploded. By autumn 1916, with more than a million deaths among its retreating armies, and terrible hardship and hunger everywhere, royalist Russia was close to crumbling. The mystical authority of the Tsar – as God's anointed, according to Orthodox belief, somehow above the corruption of worldly politics – was dangerously eroded. By making himself supreme commander of military forces, and appearing to empower both a wife who was widely perceived to have pro-German sympathies, and Grigori Rasputin (the faith healer she credited with saving the life of Alexei, the haemophiliac Tsarevich), Nicholas put his family and himself directly in the firing line. In the end, there was no one else to blame. Events then moved quickly. In December 1916 Rasputin was killed by a group led by Prince Felix Yusupov, a fabulously rich, cross-dressing charmer married to Minny's granddaughter Irina. Minny, who had moved to Kiev, may have known of the plan, and certainly approved of it afterwards. But amid all the infighting, the government was effectively paralysed, and a revolution in February 1917 forced the Tsar's abdication and detention. At Easter 1917 the Tsar and his family were under house-arrest at Tsarskoe Selo palace outside Petrograd (the anti-German name for St Petersburg since 1914), and Carl Fabergé was denied admittance. He had hoped to present a bill for 125,000 roubles, addressed to Nicholas Romanov.

FABERGÉ
French Bulldog *c.* 1910
Agate, guilloché enamel, rose diamonds
h. 98 x w. 130 x d. 61 mm
ROYAL COLLECTION TRUST

A photo in the Royal Collection shows Edward VII with Paul, a French bulldog belonging to his son, George, in 1902 – the year before the monarch single-handedly launched the Entente Cordiale. This was the first step in the Triple Entente completed with the Anglo-Russian Convention in 1907, which left Germany surrounded.

CHAPTER SIXTEEN

The Requiem

A small window opened in the spring of 1917, allowing exile for Nicholas and his family in England, but an outbreak of measles ruled out an immediate move for the children. When they recovered, the window had closed. King George V – cousin Georgie – and the Lloyd George government had panicked, fearing that sanctuary for such widely loathed autocrats might spark revolution at home. And the ousted Empress, who had thought herself so English, was reviled as a German. Her sister Elizabeth, who had married Alexander III's brother and become a nun after his 1905 assassination – giving away all her possessions, including a Fabergé collection – had already found her convent targeted in anti-German protests.

In August 1917, amid a rising tide of revolution, the Kerensky government evacuated the former royal family to Tobolsk, in the Urals. (Minny, along with daughters Xenia and Olga and their families, had already fled to safer Crimea.) After the Bolsheviks seized power in October, conditions for the detainees steadily worsened as civil war raged and the chance of rescue by royalist White forces grew. On 30 April 1918 the ex-royal family were sent to Ekaterinburg, where many Fabergé hardstones had been mined. Their destination was the Ipatiev House, which had its windows blocked by a palisade of planking, in a grotesque caricature of a romantic wooden dacha from the old days; it also gained a new name: the House of Special Purpose. Soon after midnight on 17 July the Romanovs were woken and taken to the basement where, together with four attendants, they were shot and bayoneted to death. Daughters Olga, Tatiana, Maria and Anastasia were said to have survived an initial hail of bullets, protected by gems and jewellery (very probably including pieces of Fabergé) sewn into their underclothes. The next day a group including the ex-Empress's sister, Elizabeth, and four grand dukes and

The House of Special Purpose

Nicholas, Alexandra and their children (left to right: Maria, Alexei, Olga, Tatiana, Anastasia) in 1913.

princes, were beaten and thrown down a mineshaft. The ex-Tsar's younger brother Michael, to whom Nicholas had sought to hand the crown but who had refused it pending proof of public support that never came, had been murdered a month earlier. He had been shot, together with his English secretary, in a forest in Perm.

After the October Revolution, Minny was held under house-arrest with daughter Xenia and her sons. The hated Germans arrived in April 1918, allowing greater freedom but inciting Romanov disdain, until the Bolsheviks returned with the Armistice in November. At this point Minny's position was desperate indeed. Alix, frantic with worry, wrote just before Christmas:

> *Darling Minny, have just been informed that it would be advisable for you to leave at once before more complications and horrors so please make up your mind before too late to come to me here in England at once. Bring everybody you wish, your loving sister Alix.*

Minny replied:

> *Darling Alix, thank you with all my heart for your dear telegram. Though I long to see you awfully, see no real necessity to leave now for the moment. Have written today. Loving Christmas wishes to you all.*

Finally, pressed by his mother and perhaps by his conscience for the failure to save Nicholas, Alexandra and their children, George V instructed the Admiralty to inform the Commander-in-Chief in the Mediterranean of his 'great concern' for the safety of his aunt and surviving relatives in Crimea. The message added: 'Admiralty considers situation is now such that they should be embarked whatever may be their personal desires and removed to a place of safety as soon as preparations can be made.'

When the doughty Minny at last consented to leave, in April 1919, she insisted that everyone in peril left

FABERGÉ
Three First World War Ashtrays 1914
Silver, brass, copper
Each d. 114 mm
A LA VIEILLE RUSSIE, NEW YORK

with her on any available vessel – and that she, on HMS Marlborough, should sail last of all. She also had her two Pekingese, Chi Foo and Soon, and her daughter Xenia had her dog, Toby. Grandsons brought pets Mutzi and Bobi. But due to the cramming of human passengers, a canine quota was enforced, according to size. Princess Sofka Dolgorouky, aged 11 and on board with her grandmother, Minny's best friend, had to leave behind Rim, her beloved Great Dane.

The royal refugees also departed with a mountain of precious luggage. The Yusupovs had two rolled-up Rembrandts, and the wares of Fabergé were liberally spread among the princely party. Minny left with the last of the eggs she had received almost every Easter since 1885 – 1916's *Cross of St George Egg*, bearing miniature portraits of Nicholas II and her grandson Alexei. Sold by her daughters after her death, it is now in St Petersburg's Fabergé Museum.

Having lost her favourite son to tuberculosis, Minny now refused to believe that her last two sons had been murdered, along with her daughter-in-law and five of her grandchildren. In fact 17 Romanovs had been, or would be, killed – the same number now being rescued. Minny would live for nearly another decade, never accepting the terrible truth. Instead she fretted about relative trivialities – the rigmarole of protocol and precedence. Frances Welch, Suffolk-based author of *The Russian Court at Sea: The Last Days of a Great Dynasty – The Romanovs' Voyage into Exile*, notes that Minny's 'whims had an unattractive way of growing into obsessions. But they may have been born less of entitlement than despair. After two years of torment, the Dowager was locked in a never-ending battle with the last straw.'

Although George V was happy for England to provide a refuge for his aunt and her immediate family, most of the grand dukes and duchesses were expected to quit the

FABERGÉ
Soup kettle *c.* 1914
Copper, brass
h. 140 x d. 95 mm
A LA VIEILLE RUSSIE, NEW YORK

Unknown Maker
Hand Grenade, No 34 Mark II ('Egg Grenade')
Metal
h. 100 x d. 49 mm
IMPERIAL WAR MUSEUM

The British No 34 hand grenade, known as the 'egg' grenade because of its shape, was introduced in 1917 to match German light 'egg grenades'. With a compact cast-iron body and brass striker, it was particularly suitable for trench fighting. The Russian equivalent was made in vast numbers by Fabergé.

rescue vessel in foreign ports. Fear of resentment, even revolution, still prevailed. Half the refugees were duly disembarked at Malta, where Minny and her immediate family switched to HMS Lord Nelson for the last leg of the voyage.

After the sisters enjoyed an emotional reunion at Portsmouth, before a formal reception from King George and Queen Mary at Victoria Station, Minny was taken to Sandringham to recover from her long ordeal. But she never could. Alix was deafer and more unpunctual than ever. Minny was beset by arthritis, lumbago and pain at every slight. She tried in vain to make Alix claim precedence over Mary, in the Russian manner of deference to dowagers. And it galled her that she could not even claim equality with her sister. By August she had had enough, and left for Denmark with the comment, 'Better number one at Hvidøre [the Danish villa she and her sister actually owned jointly] than number two at Sandringham.' The sisters met for the last time when Minny returned, in 1923, for the April wedding of the Duke of York – the future George VI – to Elizabeth Bowes-Lyon at Westminster Abbey. Minny fell ill, and stayed on for several months, with one last convalescent spell at Sandringham.

Alexandra died, in Norfolk, on 20 November 1925. The Duchess of York gave birth to a daughter – Elizabeth Alexandra Mary – on 21 April 1926, who would become Britain's longest-reigning monarch. Minny died in Denmark on 13 October 1928. In 2006 her remains were returned to St Petersburg and interred beside those of Alexander III in the Peter and Paul Cathedral – eight years after a reburial service for the recovered bones of the canonised Nicholas, Alexandra and their children.

Minny's elder daughter Xenia remained in England, sponsored by her British kin and living latterly at Wilderness House, Hampton Court, until her death in April 1960. The Dowager's younger daughter, Olga, had refused to escape on HMS Marlborough. She finally left Russia in February 1920. A month later Queen Alexandra unveiled the London memorial to Norfolk nurse Edith Cavell, who had been shot in Brussels in October 1915 for aiding the escape of Allied soldiers. Olga lived first with Minny, and then on farms in Denmark and Canada. She continued to paint the flower-rife watercolours so favoured at Sandringham. Famously generous, she liked visitors to leave with little gifts that might include pieces of Fabergé. Finally moving to a flat above a shop in Toronto, she died in November 1960.

The House of Fabergé fell with war and revolution. With staff drafted into the tsarist army – and the chief stone-carver an early casualty – Fabergé was doubly motivated to protect his workforce and demonstrate his patriotism by military production. A new range of cooking pots, bowls and cigarette cases in base metals could be ordered for noble sons serving on the front by parents concerned for their habitual comforts.

Sometimes an appearance of austerity was faked with silver objects gilded to look like brass. Most significantly, the Fabergé workshops came to produce millions of bullets and egg-shaped hand grenades – exquisitely designed to be absolutely lethal.

The Bolshevik Revolution followed popular revulsion over the war, and seeming to have profited from military manufacture compounded the offences of servants of the old regime. So the House of Fabergé was closed and its property confiscated. An age had truly ended.

Although Britain failed to rescue the Tsar and his immediate family, Carl Fabergé may have been disguised as a member of the British Legation while seated on the last diplomatic train to leave revolutionary Petrograd for Riga. When revolution reached Latvia, in November 1918, he fled to Germany. A month later his wife and eldest son, Eugene, escaped by sleigh and on foot through frozen woods to reach Finland. Most of the family were reunited in Switzerland, where Carl Fabergé died, still in deep shock, in 1920. Sons Alexander and Agathon had been imprisoned, though Alexander soon escaped and managed to flee abroad after bribing his guards. Agathon was released in 1921 to catalogue treasures seized from the imperial palaces, but his valuations were undercut in a global market flooded by exiles forced to sell their possessions for the essentials of life, and he was returned to jail. He and his wife and son eventually emigrated in 1928. Carl's youngest son, Nicholas, had stayed on in England during the war and after the closure of the London store in 1915. He was the luckiest of them all.

CHAPTER SEVENTEEN

A Sign of the Times

Where Alix was notoriously tardy, being late for her wedding and countless events thereafter, and rarely rising before 11am, Minny had a tyrannical approach to time: she insisted on absolute punctuality. When the Bolsheviks seized power in Russia, the sweeping away of the old order, with a switching of the capital to Moscow, would be confirmed by the imposition of a new Gregorian calendar. The symbolic leap forward of 13 days was then followed by a further onward march of two hours.

Minny had already been pitched into the future on visits to Norfolk, via an enforced adjustment to Sandringham Time. At Sandringham, clocks had always been advanced by half an hour, to maximise daylight in winter and allow more time for shooting.

For a dowager empress, and the world she came from, time was finally changed forever.

FABERGÉ
Workmaster Henrik Wigström
St. Petersburg Admiralty Clock *c.* 1910
Enamel, gold, pearls, rose diamonds
h. 108 mm
A LA VIEILLE RUSSIE, NEW YORK

This sepia enamel clock depicts St Petersburg's Admiralty. It is part of a series of objects decorated with important monuments inspired by the city's 1903 bicentenary.

Acknowledgements

I am most grateful to Sainsbury Centre director Paul Greenhalgh for hatching a fabulous enterprise with me in the wake of our *Masterpieces: Art and East Anglia* collaboration in 2013-14, in which all five featured Fabergé animals were voted among visitor favourites. Its delivery has been due to an excellent Sainsbury Centre team, and most especially to Project Curator, Claudia Milburn.

Both this book and the accompanying Royal Fabergé exhibition have depended upon the remarkable generosity of the Royal Collection Trust, and in particular I thank director Jonathan Marsden, senior curator and Fabergé expert Caroline de Guitaut and Rufus Bird, Deputy Surveyor of The Queen's Works of Art.

My earlier writing on Fabergé's Sandringham Commission may have suggested an almost random incident in the history of East Anglian art and I am now hugely indebted to three experts who have helped me to grasp the creative achievement of the workshops and the local and global context of the commission's origins and aftermath over seven decades. Cynthia Coleman Sparke, author of the splendid volume *Russian Decorative Arts*, has been my invaluable Fabergé consultant. UEA Professor Peter Waldron has been a most enlightening guide to Russia and Graham Beck has kindly shared his brilliant researches into family and Sandringham history.

By an astonishing piece of luck, Peter Schaffer of A La Vieille Russie in New York was already a friend of the Sainsbury Centre. After all his assistance throughout this adventure, he is a now a good friend of mine.

I warmly thank designer Kaarin Wall, copy editor Mandy Greenfield, our sponsors: Barratt and Cooke, Jarrold, Mills and Reeve, Lycetts, Adnams, Crabtree & Crabtree, Conrad Blakey OBE, Michael Blakey, Simon Blakey and media sponsor Russian Art and Culture. Best thanks, too, to all our lenders.

Thanks also to Professor Edward Acton, Stella Acton, Lesley Bellew, Darin Bloomquist of Sotheby's, Wendy Bonus, Jane Bulmer, David William Cripps, the Marquess of Cholmondeley, Lady Elton, Dame Elizabeth Esteve-Coll, Lady Jane Fellowes, Lord Fisher of Kilverstone, Fiona Ford, Luisa Foster, Neil Foster, Sara Foster, Jamie Freeman, Alan Fry, Marianne Fry, Amanda Geitner, the Hon Sarah Greenall, Ryan Hale, Emma Hunter, Robert Hunter, the Earl of Iveagh, Joachim Jacobs, the Right Rev. Graham James, Julie James, Caroline Jarrold, Richard Jewson, Andrew Johnson, Sheila McDonald, Laura McGillivray, Canon Michael McLean, Cathy McLennan, Francesca Makins, John Millwood, Yvonne Millwood, Munnings Art Museum at Dedham, Norfolk Wildlife Trust, Judy Novak, Nigel Orme, Kevin Parker, Anna Pavlova, Pavel Pilipenko, Harvey Pitcher, Stephanie Renouf, Nicole Roberts, Professor Keith Roberts, Andre Ruzhnikov, Olivia Stewart, Claire Tuck of Bonhams, Francesca Vanke, Moya Willson, Sofka Zinovieff and Paul Zuckerman.

FABERGÉ
Rooster 1896
Silver
l. 102 mm
A LA VIEILLE RUSSIE, NEW YORK

Picture Credits

Every effort has been made to seek permission to reproduce the images in this book and we are grateful to the individuals and institutions who have assisted us in this task. Any omissions are unintentional.
Specific acknowledgements are as follows: (A = above, B = below, L = left, C = centre, R = right)

Front/Back Cover

A La Vieille Russie, New York

Contents

5 A La Vieille Russie, New York

Introduction

7 A La Vieille Russie, New York
8 Royal Collection Trust / © Her Majesty Queen Elizabeth II 2017
9 Royal Collection Trust / © Her Majesty Queen Elizabeth II 2017

Chapter One

11 Royal Collection Trust / © Her Majesty Queen Elizabeth II 2017
13 A La Vieille Russie, New York
14 A La Vieille Russie, New York
16 Royal Collection Trust / © Her Majesty Queen Elizabeth II 2017
17 A La Vieille Russie, New York
18 A La Vieille Russie, New York

Chapter Two

20 Royal Collection Trust / © Her Majesty Queen Elizabeth II 2017
21 Royal Collection Trust / © Her Majesty Queen Elizabeth II 2017
22 A La Vieille Russie, New York
24 Private Collection. Photo: Keith Roberts
25 David William Cripps Collection
26 David William Cripps Collection
27 Royal Collection Trust / © Her Majesty Queen Elizabeth II 2017
28 Royal Collection Trust / © Her Majesty Queen Elizabeth II 2017
29A Copyright Desmond Banks. Image courtesy of Liss Llewellyn Fine Art
29B Royal Collection Trust / © Her Majesty Queen Elizabeth II 2017

Chapter Three

30 A La Vieille Russie, New York
31 A La Vieille Russie, New York
32 A La Vieille Russie, New York
33 Royal Collection Trust / © Her Majesty Queen Elizabeth II 2017
34 A La Vieille Russie, New York
35A Andre Ruzhnikov
35B Andre Ruzhnikov
36-7 A La Vieille Russie, New York
39 Gilbert Collection © The Rosalinde and Arthur Gilbert Collection on loan to the Victoria and Albert Museum, London.
40A Courtesy of the Trustees of the Royal Navy Trophy Fund
40B Andre Ruzhnikov
41 The Queen's Own Warwickshire and Worcestershire Yeomanry Regimental Charitable Trust
42 A La Vieille Russie, New York
43 © National Portrait Gallery, London

Chapter Four

44 Courtesy of Norfolk County Council Library and Information Service
45 Private Collection
46A Private Collection
46B Private Collection. Photograph courtesy of Sotheby's
47A Courtesy of the Earl of Iveagh
47B Courtesy of the Earl of Iveagh
48 By kind permission of the Marquess of Cholmondeley
49a Royal Collection Trust / © Her Majesty Queen Elizabeth II 2017
49b Royal Collection Trust / © Her Majesty Queen Elizabeth II 2017

Chapter Five

50 Norfolk Museums Service (Norwich Castle Museum & Art Gallery)
51A Royal Collection Trust / © Her Majesty Queen Elizabeth II 2017
51B Norfolk Museums Service (Norwich Castle Museum & Art Gallery)
52L Private Collection
52R Norfolk Museums Service (Norwich Castle Museum & Art Gallery)
53A Royal Collection Trust / © Her Majesty Queen Elizabeth II 2017
53B Royal Collection Trust / © Her Majesty Queen Elizabeth II 2017

Chapter Six

54L Andre Ruzhnikov
54R Andre Ruzhnikov
55 Private collection, Norfolk
56 A La Vieille Russie, New York
57 A La Vieille Russie, New York

Chapter Eight

61 A La Vieille Russie, New York
62L Private Collection
62R A La Vieille Russie, New York
63 A La Vieille Russie, New York
64A Reproduced with kind permission of the Kennel Club
64B Royal Collection Trust / © Her Majesty Queen Elizabeth II 2017
65 Royal Collection Trust / © Her Majesty Queen Elizabeth II 2017

Chapter Nine

66 Private Collection
67 © National Portrait Gallery, London

Chapter Ten

68L Royal Collection Trust / © Her Majesty Queen Elizabeth II 2017
68C Royal Collection Trust / © Her Majesty Queen Elizabeth II 2017
68R Royal Collection Trust / © Her Majesty Queen Elizabeth II 2017
69 Royal Collection Trust / © Her Majesty Queen Elizabeth II 2017
70 Royal Collection Trust / © Her Majesty Queen Elizabeth II 2017
71 A La Vieille Russie, New York
73 Royal Collection Trust / © Her Majesty Queen Elizabeth II 2017
74A Royal Collection Trust / © Her Majesty Queen Elizabeth II 2017
74B Royal Collection Trust / © Her Majesty Queen Elizabeth II 2017
75 Royal Collection Trust / © Her Majesty Queen Elizabeth II 2017
76A Royal Collection Trust / © Her Majesty Queen Elizabeth II 2017
76BL Private Collection
76BR Private Collection
77 Royal Collection Trust / © Her Majesty Queen Elizabeth II 2017
78A Royal Collection Trust / © Her Majesty Queen Elizabeth II 2017
78BL Royal Collection Trust / © Her Majesty Queen Elizabeth II 2017
78BR Royal Collection Trust / © Her Majesty Queen Elizabeth II 2017
79 Private Collection
80A Royal Collection Trust / © Her Majesty Queen Elizabeth II 2017
80B Royal Collection Trust / © Her Majesty Queen Elizabeth II 2017
81 Royal Collection Trust / © Her Majesty Queen Elizabeth II 2017
82 © National Portrait Gallery, London
83A Royal Collection Trust / © Her Majesty Queen Elizabeth II 2017
83B Royal Collection Trust / © Her Majesty Queen Elizabeth II 2017
84 Private Collection
85 Private Collection
86 Private Collection
87 Royal Collection Trust / © Her Majesty Queen Elizabeth II 2017
88 © Estate of Sir Alfred Munnings, Dedham, Essex. All rights reserved, DACS 2017
89 Royal Collection Trust / © Her Majesty Queen Elizabeth II 2017
90 Royal Collection Trust / © Her Majesty Queen Elizabeth II 2017
91L Royal Collection Trust / © Her Majesty Queen Elizabeth II 2017
91R Royal Collection Trust / © Her Majesty Queen Elizabeth II 2017
92 Royal Collection Trust / © Her Majesty Queen Elizabeth II 2017
93L A La Vieille Russie, New York
93R Royal Collection Trust / © Her Majesty Queen Elizabeth II 2017
94A A La Vieille Russie, New York
94B Royal Collection Trust / © Her Majesty Queen Elizabeth II 2017
95 Royal Collection Trust / © Her Majesty Queen Elizabeth II 2017
97 Royal Collection Trust / © Her Majesty Queen Elizabeth II 2017
98 Royal Collection Trust / © Her Majesty Queen Elizabeth II 2017
99 Royal Collection Trust / © Her Majesty Queen Elizabeth II 2017

Chapter Eleven

100 Private Collection
101 Private Collection
102 Royal Collection Trust / © Her Majesty Queen Elizabeth II 2017
103 Royal Collection Trust / © Her Majesty Queen Elizabeth II 2017

Chapter Twelve

104A Private Collection
104B Private Collection
105 Royal Collection Trust / © Her Majesty Queen Elizabeth II 2017
106 Ian Collins
107 Private Collection, Suffolk

Chapter Thirteen

108 Private Collection
109A © Victoria and Albert Museum, London.
109B © Victoria and Albert Museum, London.

Chapter Fourteen

110 Private Collection
111L Private Collection
111R Private Collection
112-3 Norfolk Museums Service (Lynn Museum)
114A Private Collection
114B Private Collection
115 Private Collection

Chapter Fifteen

116 David William Cripps Collection
117 Royal Collection Trust / © Her Majesty Queen Elizabeth II 2017
118 Private Collection, Norfolk. Photo courtesy of Bonhams
119 © Imperial War Museums (Art.IWM ART 2493)
120A Photograph courtesy Eastern Daily Press
120B Photograph courtesy Eastern Daily Press
121A Private Collection
121B Private Collection
122 Andre Ruzhnikov
123 Royal Collection Trust / © Her Majesty Queen Elizabeth II 2017

Chapter Sixteen

124 Private Collection
125 PF-(bygone1) / Alamy Stock Photo
126 A La Vieille Russie, New York
127 A La Vieille Russie, New York
128 © Imperial War Museums (MUN 3214)

Chapter Seventeen

131 A La Vieille Russie, New York

Acknowledgements

132 A La Vieille Russie, New York

Index

136 Royal Collection Trust / © Her Majesty Queen Elizabeth II 2017
137 By kind permission of the Marquess of Cholmondeley
139 Royal Collection Trust / © Her Majesty Queen Elizabeth II 2017
140L A La Vieille Russie, New York
140R A La Vieille Russie, New York

Index

Fabergé objects are among the titles in *italics*. Illustrations are in **bold**.

FABERGÉ
Guinea Pig *c.* 1907
Agate, cabochon rubies
h. 32 x w. 62 x d. 28 mm
ROYAL COLLECTION TRUST

FABERGÉ
Desk Seal
Nephrite, rose diamonds
h. 75 x w. 25 mm
PRIVATE COLLECTION, NORFOLK

FABERGÉ
Swallow *c.* 1907
Obsidian, quartzite, rose diamonds, gold
h. 25 x w. 64 x d. 16 mm
ROYAL COLLECTION TRUST

FABERGÉ
Baboon and Monkey *c.* 1900
Silver
h. 95 and 114 mm
A LA VIELLE RUSSIE, NEW YORK

These simian table lighters, with wicks in their tails, illustrate Fabergé's sense of humour. The seated Baboon is anatomically correct but Monkey is a curiosity. It most resembles a chimpanzee – though chimps in life are tail-less – but the face also recalls 19th-century caricatures of Charles Darwin mocking the author of *On the Origin of Species* as an ape.